WORKING EMPTINESS

Toward a Third Reading of Emptiness in Buddhism and Postmodern Thought

AAR

American Academy of Religion
Reflection and Theory in the Study of Religion

Editor
David E. Klemm

Number 01
WORKING EMPTINESS
Toward a Third Reading of Emptiness in
Buddhism and Postmodern Thought
by
Newman Robert Glass

WORKING EMPTINESS

Toward a Third Reading of Emptiness in Buddhism and Postmodern Thought

by
Newman Robert Glass

Scholars Press
Atlanta, Georgia

WORKING EMPTINESS

Toward a Third Reading of Emptiness in Buddhism and Postmodern Thought

by
Newman Robert Glass

Cover Photo: *Taming the Ox*, Hanging scroll by Sekkyakushi.
(Courtesy of the Asian Art Museum of San Francisco,
The Avery Brundage Collection—B69 D46.)

Library of Congress Cataloging in Publication Data
Glass, Newman Robert.
    Working emptiness : toward a third reading of emptiness in
Buddhism and postmodern thought / by Newman Robert Glass.
       p.   cm. —(AAR reflection and theory in the study of religion ;
no. 01)
    Includes bibliographical references.
    ISBN 0-7885-0080-5 (alk. paper). — ISBN 0-7885-0081-3 (pbk. :
alk. paper)
    1. Sunyata. 2. Postmodernism—Religious aspects—Buddhism.
3. Buddism and philosophy. I. Title. II. Series.
BQ4275.G57   1995
294.3'42—dc20   95-9290
                                                CIP

Printed in the United States of America
on acid-free paper
∞

The reasons for writing a book can be traced back to a desire to modify the relations that exist between a man and his fellow creatures. The extant relations are judged unacceptable and are perceived as an agonizing affliction.

-- Georges Bataille

No one can say where a book comes from, least of all the person who writes it.

-- Paul Auster

ACKNOWLEDGMENTS

I would like to thank Shotaro Iida and Dale Wright for encouragement in the initial stages of this project. The Social Sciences and Humanities Research Council of Canada provided financial support while I was doing the research for the book. Conversations with Philippa Berry, David Loy, David Miller, Ruth Ost, Richard Pilgrim and Charles Winquist have all contributed greatly to the final result. Mary Keller and Judith Poxon endured (with grace) repeated oral readings of various chapters and pressed me to further clarify my position. Although we have not met, Brian Massumi and Mark C. Taylor should also be named as among those who have shaped and sharpened my thinking on the issues of this book. Special thanks go to Nancy Baker and Ruth Tonner for their support during the completion of the manuscript. This is not to say, of course, that any of the preceding is in the slightest agreement with what follows.

TABLE OF CONTENTS

TABLE OF CONTENTS

LIST OF ILLUSTRATIONS

1 WORKING EMPTINESS

What Buddhism speaks of as enlightenment, or liberation from the craving for things, Heidegger speaks of as *Gelassenheit*, releasement from the will to power over all things.

-- Michael Zimmerman[1]

Śūnyata [emptiness] and *différance* can be understood as the differential that forms and deforms all differences. These differences, paradoxically, both constitute and subvert every identity.

-- Mark C. Taylor[2]

Two radically different views of the nature and function of emptiness are reflected in the quotations above. The enlightenment or emptiness in the first is associated with phenomenology, pure experience and presencing, while the emptiness of the second is associated with deconstruction, difference and the critique of presence. How can both be associated with Buddhism? If there is more than one understanding of the nature and function of emptiness, exactly how are they similar and how are they different? How many ways of thinking emptiness are there?

The question of whether there are various understandings of nothing or emptiness arose out of my study of Buddhism and postmodern theology. Both of these disciplines can be seen as centered on the study of "gaps" or "nothings." Yet a closer look reveals that there is no center to either discipline, and that there are serious splits within each over the nature of these "nothings."

In postmodern theology, this split can be seen in the debate between Mark C. Taylor's work on nothing as difference and Thomas J.J. Altizer's work on nothing or emptiness as "total presence." Although both work with a "logic of negation," they have opposed understandings of the working of this negation and this leads to quite different theological positions.

Within Buddhist studies this split can be seen between two opposed understandings of Nāgārjuna's equation of (co)dependent arising and *śūnyatā* or emptiness. Although both of these explications of (co)dependent arising begin

1

with a "logic of negation," they end in quite different ways, one affirmative and one negative, which, again, lead to quite different theological positions. This split is further complicated by its twofold nature: it seems to exist both in the Buddhist tradition and in the scholarly tradition which studies it.

These two workings of presence and difference are also apparent in comparative projects. For instance, if one wishes to compare Mark C. Taylor and Nāgārjuna, then a specific reading of the working of emptiness (as difference or differing) must be employed. However, if one wishes to compare Altizer's work with Nāgārjuna, then this would involve imagining emptiness at work in quite a different manner (as presence or presencing). The differences in the working of emptiness between Taylor and Altizer (difference vs. presence) seem to me to be quite similar to the differences that exist among scholars of Buddhism in reading *śūnyatā* -- negative vs. positive readings of (co)dependent arising.

Yet something crucial has been left out of both of these debates. On the postmodern side there seems the possibility of a third reading of emptiness. As Edith Wyschogrod has stated:

> . . . there are alternative strands of postmodernism. First there is the tendency in which delay and difference as disruptive of cognitive, axiological, and metaphysical wholeness are stressed. The other thread . . . posits desire as a kind of plenum with nothing to stop its headlong rush other than lines of flight that turn the plenum into its obverse [pure emptiness].[3]

This split in postmodern thought can be located between those who work with "difference" (such as Derrida, Levinas and Mark C. Taylor, who discuss otherness, gap, abyss and lack) and those who work with "positive desire" (such as Deleuze and Guattari, whose discussion of "becomings" and "plateaus of intensity" seems to call into question some of the concepts of the first group). While the philosophers of difference see "nothing" as gap, lack or difference, the philosophers of "desire" see nothingness, or emptiness, as an affective state seemingly constructed through the maintenance of "positive desire." Yet this latter notion of emptiness has not been fully developed as a position that is clearly distinct and different from the first two in its philosophical and theological implications.[4]

There are hints of a third reading of emptiness within Buddhist studies as well. The Tathāgatagarbha literature seems to contain what might be called a "*śūnyatā* of essence" which uses what Gadjin Nagao has called the logic of "subtraction," in contrast to differing uses of the logic of negation in reading (co)dependent arising.[5] This logic of subtraction yields "two wisdoms of *śūnyatā*," only the first of which can be seen as (co)dependent arising. Although scholars of Buddhism are well aware of Tathāgatagarbha thought, it has not yet been fully developed as a distinctly different third working of emptiness; it is either dismissed as somehow un-Buddhist, or understood as a variation on the first positive reading of (co)dependent arising.

Current work in postmodern theology and Buddhist studies, then, tends to emphasize two workings of emptiness or nothingness: the working of affirmation, presence or positive (co)dependent arising and the working of negation, difference or negative (co)dependent arising. There are, of course, variations in the use of each of these workings of emptiness but none of these is distinctly different in either its mode of thinking or its ethical consequences. However, both disciplines seem to contain the possibility of a third working of emptiness that is either a) not yet fully developed by scholars, or b) read in a way that it is a variation of one of the first two workings of emptiness.

This third working of emptiness, which I call "essence," accepts dependent arising, but does not see it as primary or ultimate. A distinction is made between the conventional truth of emptiness as dependent arising and the ultimate truth of emptiness as Buddha Nature or Buddha essence. In this third understanding (co)dependent arising describes the nature and function of emptiness in thinking, but not its nature and function in desire and affect. This third reading suggests that any attempt to describe emptiness in terms of thinking or objects misses the point -- emptiness needs to be approached instead in terms of affect, emotion, force or desire.

From the perspective of this third position, Buddha essence, the debate between the two (co)dependent arising readings is a disagreement over the nature and function of emptiness in thinking, a disagreement which fails to attend to what is primary -- the nature and function of emptiness in desire and affect. From this perspective, Buddhist practice is best understood not as a move from thinking to non-thinking, but as a move from craving to compassion. Emptiness is not an achieved state of thinking (without thinking) but an achieved state of desire (compassion).

This book then has two goals: first, to be specific in articulating the different dimensions of the first two workings of emptiness, presence and difference -- each associated with a different reading of (co)dependent arising -- and second, to provide a reading of the third working of emptiness (essence) that is clearly distinct from the previous two. The thesis is that there are three workings of emptiness capable of grounding thinking and behaviour: the working of presence, the working of difference and the working of subtraction/essence. Further, this third working of emptiness is capable of supporting a philosophical or theological position quite distinct from the first two. The fifth chapter is an attempt to construct just such a position, hence the subtitle of the book -- toward a third reading of emptiness.

1.1 Thinking Emptiness

This book is most comparable in its approach to recent work being done under the title of "postmodern theology" within the field of the philosophy of religion. The concept of "thinking about thinking," so central to the framing of my argument, figures heavily in the work of Robert Scharlemann and Mark C. Taylor. In addition, the "what" and "how" structure of the introduction is very much indebted to Richard Grigg's *Theology as a Way of Thinking.*[6] As Grigg argues, the issue is not only "what" is thought but "how" one thinks about what is thought. Further, how one thinks about something inevitably influences and becomes part of what one is thinking. Put in terms of my own thesis, the issue is not only "emptiness" and how one thinks emptiness, but the specific relation between thinking and emptiness, and the nature and function of emptiness within the thinking process itself. Thinking and emptiness are reciprocally related, one implicating the other, and cannot be separated.

The first part of the book, then, is an exercise in comparative thinking focusing on the relationship between "thinking" and "emptiness." It attempts to investigate this relationship first by examining emptiness or nothingness as a subject of thinking, and which therefore follows thinking as one of any number of topics which thinking might address; and second, by examining emptiness or nothingness as a "space" or "clearing" that precedes thinking, as a condition of the possibility of the thinking process itself.

Thus, on the one hand, this project might be seen as a traditional exercise in comparative philosophy: What do different thinkers have to say about nothingness or emptiness? The strategy here is to approach the working of emptiness through Heidegger, Mark C. Taylor and Dōgen Kigen. These three thinkers are useful, rather than some others, for two reasons: first, because they are each particularly precise and thorough in the articulation of their thinkings; second, and more importantly, because their modes of thought have been linked in conflicting ways to Buddhist emptiness.

With respect to the individual thinkers, the book asks: What template -- or structure of thinking -- does each thinker bring to an interpretation of emptiness? How does that shape the way each "thinks emptiness"? And how might this structure of thinking skew readings of emptiness in the work of other writers? For instance, if Heideggerian thinking is used in reading about Buddhist emptiness, then is it not probable that we will end up with a Buddhist emptiness that is very similar to Heidegger's nothingness? From this perspective, then, the book stands or falls on its ability to articulate structures of thinking in Heidegger, postmodern theology and Buddhism that are clearly distinct from one another.

Yet, on the other hand, the book is not concerned with specific thinkers at all, but with examining what remains when thinking has been reduced to its "origin": emptiness. What is the nature of the emptiness from which thinking proceeds? How does emptiness function both in and apart from thinking?

Pressing the investigation into different structures of thinking encourages a re-working of the relationship between thinking and emptiness and exposes a second concern of the book. "Emptiness" or "nothingness" is not only a subject that can be addressed by thinking, but seems to function in all three thinkers as an inherent part of the thinking process itself. From this perspective the different thinkers are important only to the degree that they illustrate and help define the different workings of emptiness. There are three possible workings of emptiness, each distinct from the other in the way they orient thinking, seeing, sensing and behaviour, and the three theorists serve only as examples of these workings. From this perspective, the book is as much constructive as it is descriptive. The attempt to develop the third reading of emptiness in chapter five is best seen as an exercise in Buddhist constructive philosophy, or perhaps even Buddhist postmodern theology.

1.2 The Working of Emptiness, Without Thinking, the Unthought

Dōgen Kigen's understanding of "thinking" in the practice of meditation can be of help in clarifying my use of the phrase "the working of emptiness." He introduces the practice of meditation by splitting "thinking" into three possibilities: thinking, not thinking, and without thinking.[7] Meditation practice is the cultivation of the third of these possibilities. It is neither the act of thinking, nor the deliberate act of not thinking. Meditation is, rather, an exercise of without thinking when one lets go of thoughts as they arise, neither clinging to them nor pushing them away. Nonetheless, even when there are no thoughts, an attitude or principle remains which not only guides the functioning or working of without thinking but organizes sense and perception as well. Something is active in without thinking. What might this be? How might different ways of without thinking work? What is at work or working in emptiness?

Another way of looking at the working of emptiness is to see it in terms of the Heideggerian "unthought." Heidegger has said that a thinker's greatest thought is best understood as not a thought at all, but an unthought.   In *What is called thinking?*, he states:

> To acknowledge and respect consists in letting every thinker's thought come to us as something in each case unique, never to be repeated, inexhaustible - and being shaken to the depths by what is unthought in his thought. What is unthought in a thinker's thought is no lack inherent in his thought. What is un-thought is there in each case only as the un-thought. The more original the thinking, the richer will be what is unthought in it. The unthought is the greatest gift that thinking can bestow.[8]

The un-thought, the not-a-thought that is a condition of thought, can be seen as a "nothing" or "emptiness." But again, this unthought or emptiness is not neutral. The nature or functioning of this emptiness (the un-thought) determines the nature of what shall be thought -- not, of course, the subject matter to which it turns, but the structure of thinking itself by which the subject matter will be organized, arranged or oriented. In this sense, the one great thought of each thinker is then the specificity and working of an unthought, his or her own particular working of emptiness. This unthought is a "pre-form," and the working of this pre-form can be appreciated indirectly through the myriad forms to which it gives appearance.

The nature of the un-thought, the nothing or emptiness, is crucial in thinking. Although it seems one can choose to think anything with the Heideggerian unthought, this anything will forever be shaped by the working of the Heideggerian unthought. That is, the nature of whatever is thought is inevitably regulated and governed by the specificity of that which grounds thinking. But this book also explores a further consequence: some subject matter will not be within the realm of choice. It will remain un-thought (not addressed by thought) because of the nature of the un-thought (the working of emptiness which conditions thought); not because one chooses not to think it, but because the thinking process itself, governed as it is by the working of a specific unthought/pre-thought/emptiness, precludes perceiving or formulating it.

An earlier example may now need to be re-phrased. Perhaps the problem is not with the Heideggerian thinking of Buddhist emptiness, but with the Heideggerian un-thinking of Buddhist emptiness. If the Heideggerian "un" is used, then whatever is subsequently thought will be oriented, organized and governed by the Heideggerian unthought (whether or not Heideggerian language and concepts are used explicitly).

1.3 Desire, Affect and Emptiness

The work of emptiness investigated here manifests itself as much in seeing and sensing as it does in thinking. A change in the working of emptiness involves a change in the way one sees, draws and senses inasmuch as the work of emptiness is located at the origin of the thinking-seeing, thinking-sensing process. Therefore, while this project was initially framed in terms of thinking and emptiness, the working of emptiness should be understood to include visual and affective dimensions. Indeed, in the third reading emptiness it is a transformed affective dimension that becomes primary in the decision-making process.

From this third perspective, emptiness has less to do with thinking and seeing than it has to do with desire and affect. However, as all thinking is embodied, the nature of bodily affect has an impact on thinking and decision-making.

Consider one very simple example of the impact of forms of desire on thinking, advice on how to be thrifty in shopping for groceries: Don't shop when you are hungry. What does this suggest? It suggests that the nature of the one's bodily cravings or desire may have a powerful effect on the decisions one makes in the grocery store. The claim is this: people do not always act in their own best interests. Force, desire and craving have an impact on decision-making. In an age plagued by seemingly endless forms of both addiction and abuse, newspapers carry stories daily of people who knowingly act against their own best interests. This is not a failure of rationality but an inability to overcome different forms of force, desire and craving in living one's life. The third reading of emptiness suggests that the nature of bodily desire or craving will have a powerful effect on the decisions one makes in daily life.

In order to explore the role of desire and affect -- drive, force or emotion -- in the work of emptiness, various terms will be gathered under the heading of "sense": direction, grain, cause, bias. In the French language *sens* is almost interchangeable with "direction." A one way street is *sens unique; dans le sens* means "with the grain." The skilled woodworker works with the grain (*dans le sens*) to allow the potential of the wood to emerge. Is there a grain to emptiness? Or, when emptiness works, what is its grain, its direction, its sense?

Mark Taylor notes a useful term for exploring sense or force in his chapter on Jacques Lacan in *Altarity*. Lacan suggests there may be a "clinamen" (a leaning, inclination, or tendency) in the nothing. In a footnote to Lacan's use of clinamen Taylor refers the reader to Harold Bloom's use of the same term.[9] Bloom, in turn, acknowledges an earlier use of clinamen as a critical term in Samuel Taylor Coleridge's *Aids to Reflection*.[10] In commenting on humility, Coleridge writes:

Where there is no working of self-love in the heart that secures a leaning beforehand; where the great magnet of the planet is not overwhelmed or obscured by partial masses of iron in close neighborhood to the compass of judgment, though hidden or unnoticed; there will this great *desideratum* be found of a child-like humility. Do I then say that I am to be influenced by no interest? Far from it! . . . It is enough if the *lene clinamen*, the gentle bias, be given by no interest that concerns myself other than as I am a man, and included in the great family of mankind;[11]

Coleridge's clinamen is a leaning, a "gentle bias." Bias suggests "bent of mind" but also, in bowling, a "weight in the side of a ball that causes it to curve in its course."[12] In an attempt to explore the sense or weight of the affective dimension of the working of emptiness, terms such as direction, grain, bias, and clinamen will be employed.

Because both Heidegger and Taylor work with art to represent their understanding of emptiness, I will explore how art figures in the visual aspect of working emptiness. In my view it is possible, by reading backwards, to learn much about the way emptiness is working (and being worked) in a given thinker from the paintings that are chosen to illustrate his or her thought, and how these paintings are read. An artist draws lines and figures with a pencil or brush to make a sketch or paint, but also draws forth from what is present in order to work. The second sense of draw may even precede the first: drawing forth precedes drawing upon. Works of art can then be seen as the manifestation of an artist's orientation of his or her world.

As the artist draws in creating a painting, the viewer/theorist(whether Taylor or Heidegger) also draws in seeing the painting. Drawing precedes painting and the viewing of that which is painted. It is not only possible but probable that these two drawings (that of the artist and that of the viewer) will not be the same. One may then need a "viewer response" theory to complement "reader response" theory–the working of emptiness has a visual manifestation.

1.4 Methodology

I work within the understanding of contemporary critical theory that there may well be more than one legitimate reading of a text. This understanding of multiple readings is not a problem if everyone is part of the same interpretive community. However, the scholarly world is not an undivided whole, and different groups of scholars seem to operate under different interpretive assumptions. While there are distinctly different readings of Heidegger, there seems to be some resistance to accepting distinctly different readings of Buddhist thinkers such as Dōgen. An interpretive gap seems to exist between groups which emphasize critical theory and groups which focus on sacred texts. The interpretive assumptions of the former (e.g. scholars of postmodern thought), may seem in some sense heretical to the latter (e.g. scholars of Buddhism).[13] This may be because many religious texts have a relationship with a community of believers who, at least to a degree, organize their lives around the interpretation of these texts. A new and distinctly different interpretation of a sacred text may, then, have far more dramatic consequences than, say, a new interpretation of Heidegger.

Let me lay out the assumptions which govern my own interpretive position and argue briefly for the appropriateness of this position with regard to both philosophical and religious texts. These assumptions are partially summed up in the statement: There is no neutral surface upon which a text can be received and there can be no neutral readers of texts, whether Eastern or Western, ancient or modern, secular or sacred. Sacred texts cannot somehow stand on their own without interpretation as proof of an objective truth (or even an "objective truth") in a religious tradition. All data are in some sense fictive because before we can think them, they must first be selected, arranged and brought to understanding.

My attempt here is not to "get back to the real truth" of what emptiness is, but to explore interpretive frameworks within which this term seems to work, and be worked, differently. With this in mind, I ask the following questions:

i. What is our agenda in selecting from what we read? Why do we underline some sections of a text and not others?

ii. In what personal context are these words of the text being received and arranged? If Dōgen's words, for example, can be seen as slides, then these slides look different when they are shown on different surfaces. How am I bringing these words together with what I already understand?

One receives the words of Nāgārjuna or Dōgen within a personal interpretive framework that suggests one meaning to us rather than another. For instance, in answer to the question: "What is the genuine meaning of śūnyatā?" one Buddhist scholar may choose a line in Nāgārjuna while another will choose a line from the *Ratnagotra*. This is clearly not an objective or neutral decision and has important consequences. Further, even when a similar choice is made, the same text can mean many different things when read by scholars of different interpretive frameworks. There is a critical difference between what Nāgārjuna (or Dōgen) "said" and what scholars may understand these statements to "mean." The first point is an issue of agreeing on a common translation. The second point is agreeing on what this common translation means. The issue, again, is that it is entirely possible for two scholars to have opposed readings of the same text.[14]

Even after a "fact" has been chosen, it takes on meaning only when put in some context or tied together with some narrative thread. Different contexts can give the same fact quite different meanings. In the end, one cannot separate ancient texts from modern day commentators, for it is clearly present day scholars who choose the texts, place them in a particular context or narrative web, and then interpret their specifics. The same text can be (and has been) used to support two completely different workings of emptiness.

In light of this, this book is best seen not as a project investigating questions such as "What did Dōgen (or Heidegger, etc.) say?" -- but as a project more concerned with "How are we understanding what Dōgen said?" or "Upon what surfaces are Dōgen's words being received and how does each surface alter our understanding?" (What logic is being used in reading and understanding Dōgen?) Each reading has different implications for understanding Dōgen (different surfaces yield different Dōgens) and each has different consequences for the question of ethics. However, although a text may have multiple readings, it cannot mean anything one wishes. All readings must meet certain minimal standards of comprehensiveness, consistency and explanatory power. Further, in the case of Dōgen, a position on any one issue (meditation, ethics, karma, emptiness, enlightenment) inevitably commits one to a similar position on all the others.

Thomas Kuhn sums up lessons learned in trying to read ancient texts in the history of science as follows:

> First, there are many ways to read a text, and the ones most accessible to a modern are often inappropriate when applied to the past. Second, the plasticity of texts does not place all ways of reading on a par, for some of them (ultimately, one hopes, only one) possess a plausibility and coherence absent from others. Trying to transmit such lessons to students, I offer them a maxim: When reading the works of an important thinker, look first for the apparent absurdities in the text and ask how a sensible person could have written them. When you find an answer, I continue, when those passages make sense, then you may find that more central passages, ones you thought you understood, have changed their meaning.[15]

Although reading Heidegger or Dōgen is clearly different from reading in the history of science, I think this strategy has much to recommend it. Kuhn's point that there may be a need for a shift in thinking on the part of the reader is a crucial one, and lies at the heart of my argument for a third reading of emptiness.

However, a shift in thinking may not be a shift in "unthinking" -- a shift in the working of the "unthought" that determines thought. In the end, this book, as well, falls into only one "un" and is inevitably flawed in a way similar to those attempts at comparative thinking it criticizes. (One wonders in which way the Heideggerian thinking - or "unthinking" of Buddhist emptiness is different from the "Glassian unthinking" of Heidegger.) As Bernard Faure puts it in relation to Buddhist studies:

> . . . scholarship -- even in its most "scientific" garb (philology, historiography, structuralism) -- has a performative function. Consequently, it has to abandon its truth claims and remain content with simply offering yet another local (and localized) reading (or performance) of the tradition -- and hoping it will prove temporarily fruitful. . . . there is no return to the Eden of candid scholarship, and Chan scholarship, like the Chan tradition itself, is condemned to develop (or perhaps to thrive) in the dialogical oscillation between hermeneutics and rhetoric, between "objectivity" and imagination.[16]

Perhaps this book, too, is the product of an "oscillation between . . . 'objectivity' and imagination." The attempt is to represent each thinker according to his own "un" (emptiness), while realizing that any such attempt must necessarily be "twisted." Yet, following Faure, perhaps it is exactly in this "twisting" that this project (or any other), may make a unique contribution.

1.5 The Question of Ethics

Emptiness is not morally neutral. If emptiness is understood to precede thinking, then the specific functioning of this emptiness will determine not only the structure in which one thinks but also which choices will be available for thinking to consider. From this perspective the work of emptiness has ethical consequences as it determines which choices present themselves in considering patterns of action.

However, this is a use of the term "ethics" which addresses the nature of thinking (or the nature of that which precedes thinking) rather than the specifics of behaviour. Approaching ethics through codes of behaviour, the usual strategy in comparative studies, leads to questions such as, "How do the Buddhist precepts compare to the Christian commandments?" Approaching ethics through thinking (or pre-thinking) leads to different questions. For example, "What is at work in a realization of Buddhist emptiness and what actions would be consistent with this working?" Differences in decision-making may well result from differences in the construction of perception/thinking. "Ethics" in this discussion is then an analysis of the availability of options (what is it that makes some choices available and not others?) rather than an analysis of the means for choosing between options. There is a step back from rules the thinking process might follow to what underlies the thinking process itself. What is the nature of that which is prior to thought? And how might this govern behaviour?

The inquiry into the link between emptiness and a ground for ethics can be seen to be historically situated at the end of the twentieth century from the standpoint of each of the three thinkers. With regard to postmodern theology, the book might be seen as an investigation of the "ground" for action after the "death of God" or the "end of metaphysics." As Richard Kearney has put the question:

> . . . does not the postmodern tendency to collapse the old oppositions between truth and falsehood, the real and the imaginary, the authentic and the mythical, not preclude the possibility of ethical judgement and critical discernment?[17]

> . . . the poetical readiness to tolerate the undecidability of play must be considered in relation to the ethical readiness to decide between different modes of response to the other. . . [18]

Kearney pinpoints the crucial question: after the traditional basis for ethics has dissolved, after ethics itself has been deconstructed, what is the legitimizing "ground" of thought and action? On what basis does one make choices? Given emptiness, whither ethics?

With reference to Buddhism, emptiness has taken on a new importance and has raised new questions in the move to North America. The interest in Buddhism in general, and in Dōgen's emptiness in particular, arises in the context of what many regard as a moral vacuum. A focus of attention then becomes the Buddhist concept of nothingness or emptiness and the possibilities it may offer for guiding decision-making. One wonders: Is there an ethical edge in emptiness?

With reference to Heidegger, presence and "nothing," the question of Nazism has come to the foreground in academic debates. A flurry of recent texts and articles have re-examined Heidegger's personal life and its connections to his philosophical thinking. At the most extreme (and provocative) end of the spectrum are the statements of those such as Victor Farias, summarized in the introduction to his controversial *Heidegger and Nazism*. He writes that through the link to National Socialism, Heidegger "found a way to link himself and his past to the past of an entire epoch, and that, through that link as well, one could trace the subsequent evolution of Heidegger's thought in an essential way."[19] In Farias' reading, there is a link between what is essential in Heidegger's thought and Nazism itself.

At the other end of the spectrum, a question closer to the investigations of this book has been articulated by William Richardson, who asks:

> ... what was there in the thought itself ... that offered any measure, or guide, for action? Given that the essence of truth includes both mystery and errancy, the scandal is not that Heidegger skidded into Nazism; the scandal is that there was nothing in his thought ... to prevent it.[20]

Of course, these questions are not just questions about Heidegger but about this kind of thinking in general. One might ask: Are all criticisms of Heidegger's actions equally criticisms of those who model their thinking after his, who use or appropriate the Heideggerian unthought?   What about all those thinkers who acknowledge Heidegger as a formative influence in their own work? The list is long: Tillich, Gadamer, Ricoeur in one stream; Derrida and Mark C. Taylor in another. Are all these thinkers indicted as well, at least to some degree?

But the question needs to be broadened still further. Is the indictment of Heideggerian "nothing-based" thinking also in some way an indictment of all "nothing-based" thinkings? If scholars identify significant similarities between Heidegger and Buddhism, is not Buddhist thinking equally guilty of the ethical ambivalence with which Heidegger has been charged? His writings figure prominently in the Kyoto school of Japanese Buddhist philosophy; Heideggerian thinking is frequently used as an interpretive tool in understanding Dōgen's thought. Is Dōgen's thought then vulnerable to the same charges as Heidegger's? Is it simply an historical accident that scholars are not now discussing "Dōgen and Nazism"? Again, one wonders: to what degree is the working of emptiness in Heidegger, postmodern theology and Buddhism (Dōgen Kigen) the same or different? And if different, exactly how so?

My claim is that there are three workings of emptiness capable of grounding thinking and behaviour, and that the third has the potential of supporting a philosophical or theological position radically different from the first two. The first two readings present opposing views of the work of emptiness in thinking, while the third reading presents a position on the work of emptiness in desire and affect. In chapters two and three I present and analyze the two emptinesses already working, and being worked, in philosophical and religious discourse (presence and difference), and link them to their corresponding positions in Buddhism (co-dependent and dependent arising); in chapter four I argue for a third working of emptiness (essence); in chapter five I work the edge in this third emptiness in order to construct a comprehensive Buddhist position based in desire and affect, a Buddhism of essence; in chapter six, by way of summary, I compare and contrast the three workings of emptiness -- presence, difference and essence.

2 THE WORKING OF PRESENCE: HEIDEGGER, PRESENCE AND CO-DEPENDENT ARISING

The openness of the clearing of concealment is thus originally not the mere emptiness of being unoccupied, but rather the attuned and attuning emptiness of the a-byss.[21]

... the path of thinking, speculative and intuitive, needs the traversable opening. But in that opening rests possible radiance, that is, the possible presencing of presence itself.[22]

There is a remarkable affinity between Heidegger's representational and calculative thinking and Dōgen's ordinary, discriminating mind (*citta*), and between Heidegger's meditative thinking and Dōgen's Buddha-mind.[23]

Heidegger uses a number of terms to discuss the nature and functioning of emptiness (*die Leere*) or the nothing (*das Nichts*). These terms are similar, but not synonymous, in meaning and work together to bring out different nuances of his thinking on the relationship between thinking and emptiness. Emptiness as a structure, location, or product is suggested with terms such as abyss, clearing or opening (*die Lichtung*) and the Open (*das Offene*), while the activity of emptiness is suggested with terms such as releasement (*Gelassenheit*) and appropriation (*Ereignis*). Some terms, such as clearing, opening, lighting and presence, or presencing, seem to perform double duty as nouns and verbs and suggest that emptiness should be seen as both product and process. In the first quotation above Heidegger describes emptiness as both attuned and attuning. In another location Heidegger states that "nothing itself nihilates."[24]

While a number of these terms could have been chosen as an umbrella word to describe the working of emptiness in this chapter, I have decided upon "presence," or "presencing," for two reasons. First, "presence" embraces the tension between the two forms of "work," product and process, noun and verb: there is both "a presence" and "to presence." This tension, crucial to Heidegger's thinking, is apparent in the second quotation above when Heidegger states that ". . . in that opening rests possible radiance, that is, the possible presencing of presence itself."

Second, the postmodern critique of presence is now part of the context within which the term "presence" is received. "Presence" has become a general term used to characterize the work of a variety of thinkers: Husserl, Ricoeur, and Gadamer within phenomenology and hermeneutics; Thomas J. J. Altizer in postmodern theology; and Keiji Nishitani within Buddhism are among those who have been so classified. The consistent critique of presence could be seen as one of the defining characteristics of the postmodern theology of Mark C. Taylor discussed in the next chapter. (The pioneering, and still dominant, figure in this field is, of course, Jacques Derrida.) It seems important, in light of this critique, to re-examine the term in the context of Heidegger's own writings.

This chapter will attempt to clarify the nature and functioning of emptiness and presence in Heidegger by approaching them through three overlapping areas of his work: first, through thinking and Heidegger's work on what is prior to thought; second, through seeing and Heidegger's use of visual examples in his work; and third, through saying and the later Heidegger's work on (and with) language. The chapter will conclude by exploring the link between Heideggerian presencing, Buddhist meditation and the doctrine of co-dependent arising.

2.1 Thinking and Presence

> Scientist: Now authentic releasement consists in this: that man in his
> very nature belongs to that-which-regions, i.e., he is released to it.
> Scholar: Not occasionally, but -- how shall we say it -- prior to everything.
> Scientist: The prior, of which we really can not think . . .
> Teacher: . . . because the nature of thinking begins there.
> Scientist: Thus man's nature is released to that-which-regions in what is
> prior to thought.[25]

The region or realm in thinking to be explored in Heidegger can be located with the question: What is prior to thought? Because Heidegger approaches (and forms) this realm slightly differently at different times in his career, more than one approach may be necessary in order to explore its nature and functioning (that is, its working).

Let me first attempt to approach Heidegger's "prior to thought" through the notion of *Gelassenheit*. The translation of *Gelassenheit* into English is not easy. According to T.P. Kasulis, although *Gelassenheit* is usually translated into a single word as "releasement," it is perhaps more accurate to think of it as "a state of composure arising out of an attitude of letting things be."[26] Heidegger's releasement is "beyond the distinction between activity and passivity."[27] It is not a willful act. *Gelassenheit* is a stepping back into a clearing or opening where the play between thing and nothing may be sensed. This is a spacing in which there is no "thing" in the usual sense; it might be called a spacing or clearing of no thingness. Thinking must therefore occur in an area or location of no thing, and in a manner in which there is no "thinging." The origin of thinking is, therefore, a "before" of the things that are thing and nothing.

Heidegger uses the term *Gelassenheit* in relation to what he calls meditative thinking. He makes a distinction between objectifying and non-objectifying thinking, or calculative, representational thought and meditative, essential thought. Calculative thinking reckons, accounts and feels free to manipulate what is present, while meditative thinking is more a letting be, an allowing what is present to appear. The first type of thinking is associated with scientific-technological work while the second is associated more with artistic and poetic work.

Heidegger discusses the difference between calculative and meditative thinking in *Discourse on Thinking*. As Heidegger states:

> It computes ever new, ever more promising and at the same time more economical possibilities. Calculative thinking races from one prospect to the next. Calculative thinking never stops, never collects itself. Calculative thinking is not meditative thinking, not thinking which contemplates the meaning which reigns in everything that is.[28]

Calculative thinking, as a thinking that "computes," is thus opposed to meditative thinking. Calculative or representational thought is associated with Heidegger's term "framing," while meditative thought is associated with Heidegger's terms "releasement" and "appropriation."

Meditative thinking is not a "floating" thinking which "loses touch."[29] It requires work, and may even demand more effort and practice than calculative thinking. As Heidegger states, in meditative thinking we "dwell on what lies close... upon what concerns us, each one of us, here and now."[30]

In *Discourse on Thinking,* Heidegger moves from discussing releasement to a conversation on the "region in which everything returns to itself."[31] This "region" soon becomes "that-which-regions." Heidegger observes:

> So the region itself is at once an expanse and an abiding. It abides into the expanse of resting. It expands into the abiding of what has freely turned toward itself. In view of this usage of the word, we may also say "that-which-regions" in the place of the familiar "region."[32]

Again, there is a tension in the prior to thought between noun and verb, location and activity: the expanse "expands" and the region "regions."

Heidegger goes on to introduce "waiting," which he describes as a release "into the openness of that-which-regions."[33]   To sum up, in this first approach to what is prior to thought, Heidegger advocates a meditative thought practiced through "letting be" or "waiting upon," which is a release to an openness or "that-which-regions in what is prior to thought."[34]

A second approach to what is prior to thought in Heidegger is through the statement "questioning is the piety of thinking," where piety here means obedient, or perhaps obedience.[35] Questioning is the obedience of thinking. But questioning here must be understood in a way that is consistent with meditative or non-objectifying thinking. As Heidegger has stated, there is a problem with some sorts of questioning, as they can be assertions of a particular thinking framework. If questioning is done is this way it loses its quality of listening. Questioning must be pursued in such a way that listening is maintained.

Heidegger's examples of the woodworker and the traveler can be used to develop this point.[36]   The woodworker learns to be sensitive to the particularities of each piece of wood, and to allow what is best in it to guide his or her skill. Part of thinking, then, is being open, or opening, to the potential of the particular. The traveler is one who sets out on a never-ending journey. This is not a negative image but a positive one, for the purpose of traveling is never to arrive but always to be on the way. Part of the definition of thinking, then, is always being open or opening to the next step. With reference to obedience, a woodworker is one who is obedient to the wood while the traveler is one who is obedient to the nature and direction of the path. Questioning arises from a waiting upon that is sensitive to the particular.

Questioning is not an act (as in "putting" a question) but a state of thinking that is always opening. If Being can be seen as Opening, then questioning is opening (not an opening) to Opening.[37] However, since the former (questioning) can never be large enough to encompass the latter (Being), questioning always continues. A thinking that is a "thanking" gestures towards Opening in its own opening.

A third approach to thinking in Heidegger is through his use and development of hermeneutics. In the "Dialogue on Language," the question of hermeneutics arises and ends up being a natural part of the conversation on language. Language is the relation between Being and beings, but how should one understand these words "relation" and "between?"[38] Hermeneutics is not so much the interpretation of that language, but a step back from interpretation in an effort to examine the conditions in which the "between" of language arises. If language is the "house of being," then any discussion of different language "houses" must also be a discussion of hermeneutics, or the conditions under which the "house" is constructed. The word is the condition of the coming together of thing and nothing. Word draws the thing out of nothing. However, if Being and being are to be kept in balance, then the thinking and saying of the word must be done with great care, for how one uses language has an effect upon the balance between the two.

Words are then not only a "what" but a "how." Better, before words are a "what" they are a "how." To put it another way, before the question "What does that sentence mean?" there is the question "How, or on what basis, is that sentence coming into existence?" The two-fold nature of every sentence embraces a going-in and a coming-out: an oscillation.[39] Something is received before it can come out in a particular form. And, of course, a previous coming-out influences the manner of the going-in which follows. It may be that the "dialogue" in "A Dialogue on Language" is not between Heidegger and a Japanese, but between "*that which speaks*" and "those who seemingly are the only speakers -- men,"[40] between presence and present beings.

In this sense a question (any question) is not a question but a revelation. One might ask: what does the question reveal if one is listening? What does it say about thinking, nothing and presence? Hermeneutics is then an investigation of the specific character of the thinking in which the reciprocal relationship of going-in and coming-out exists. This going-in and coming-out is the oscillation of presencing. It is through this act of oscillation that opening is maintained and presencing occurs. "There is presence only when opening is dominant."[41]

It may be, though, that this point of oscillation shifts as Heidegger's thinking matures. In the attempt to think about nothing, nothing may recoil and have an effect on thinking. As Heidegger has put it:

> For thinking, which is essentially always thinking about something,
> would, in thinking of Nothing, be forced to act against its own nature.[42]

Thinking and nothing have a reciprocal effect upon one another involving both in a process of change. Heidegger seems to move from an earlier sense of hermeneutics, in which he talks about the nature of language and interpretation, to a later sense in which hermeneutics is not so much explicitly discussed as practiced. "Talking about" hermeneutics and nothing gives way to attempts at expression, or "saying." Perhaps, then, Heidegger's whole project might be seen as a move from representational or calculative hermeneutics to essential or meditative hermeneutics.

2.2 Seeing and Presence

The visual examples Heidegger chooses to illustrate his lectures are useful in attempting to understand the nature and functioning of what is prior to thought. These different examples come together to give a picture of the lines upon which his thinking and seeing are organized. In examining these Heideggerian lines one begins to see that a unique cission takes place in his thinking. Heidegger cuts, or "cises" when thinking and seeing, and does so in consistent ways.

"Cise" here is a rendering of the French word *taille*, which can be used to mean height or size, or to mean cutting, hewing, carving or engraving. In their translation of Derrida's *The Truth in Painting*, Bennington and McLeod maintain these two senses by translating *taille* as "cise."[43] In English, this "cise" combines size, as in "What size clothes do you wear?" with the sense of cission in some words such as scissors or incision. A tailor is one who uses both meanings of "cise" at once. He or she cises you as you enter the shop so that later the clothing will fit well.

Within the history of art cising can be understood in terms of the difference between Expressionist painters (such as Van Gogh or Cézanne) and Impressionist painters (such as Monet). Expressionist paintings are marked by their bold use of colour and deep black borders. One might say that they are deeply committed to cission: they cut or cise boldly in organizing their reality on canvas. In contrast to this, Impressionist paintings are not known for their use of black and might exemplify a non-cising approach to organizing perception.

Take, for example, Monet's series on the Rouen cathedral. He seems not to paint the cathedral but rather what intervenes between the eye and the cathedral. There is a dissolution of subject matter, an absence of individuality in these paintings. The painting might be as much about air and light as it is about a traditional subject. There is a very limited use of black, and a relative absence of shadow (for how can there be a shadow when there is no subject?). The power of any specific image is diffused: intensity resides not in the subject but instead in the total scene. Impressionist artists may paint the same images as the Expressionists, but, if they do so, they will render them differently. Without the use of black outline and clear edges, the images do not seem "cut" or cised.

With this in mind, Heidegger's choice and use of a Van Gogh painting to illustrate "The Origin of the Work of Art" tells much about the cuts or lines in his thinking and seeing. With reference to Van Gogh's painting of peasant shoes,

Heidegger writes that "there is nothing surrounding this [Van Gogh's] pair of peasant shoes in or to which they might belong -- only an undefined space."[44] But it is the undefined space, the nothing, that serves as boundary for the shoes. Boundary has a crucial function. It "brings to its radiance what is present. Boundary sets free into the unconcealed; by its contour in the Greek light the mountain stands in its towering and repose."[45] In Van Gogh's shoes it is the activity of the nothing that allows the shoes to shine forth in their radiant presence.[46] Nothing has an active, complementary role in creating the tension which brings forth the vitality of Being. Being is intensified in relationship with nothing. This intensification is apparent in the deeply cised borders of Van Gogh's shoes or the Greek mountain which stands against the light. This seems to me to be a decidedly Expressionist rendering of thinking and nothing.

At this point Heideggerian thinking and nothing seem to be interdependent. Thinking is not apart from nothing but determines its characteristics. Nothing allows thinking to be what it is. One cannot be changed without the other. Both are characterized by Heidegger's unique pattern of deep cission: visual cission allows the thing to stand forth in relationship to nothing; existential cission allows the person to stand forth in relationship to the nothingness of anxiety or death.

Heidegger's use of the jug example in his 1950 essay "The Thing" can be read in a similar way. Heidegger writes:

When we fill the jug, the pouring that fills it flows into the empty jug. The emptiness, the void, is what does the vessel's holding. The empty space, this nothing of the jug, is what the jug is as a holding vessel.[47]

It is not the jug that holds the wine, it is the nothing. The potter does not so much shape the jug as bring forth the nothing.

It seems probable that the formulation of this jug-nothing, written in 1950, was influenced by Heidegger's work on a translation of the *Tao Te Ching* in the summer of 1946.[48] Heidegger's use of the jug resembles many of the examples used in the presentation of Tao as function in chapter eleven of the *Tao Te Ching*. In chapter eleven reality is likened to a wheel with 30 spokes, a clay vessel, and a room with doors and windows. Although all these objects have a solid, physical form, it is on the no-thingness that the use of that form depends. In other words, the utility of the clay vessel is not in the clay, but in the space it envelops.

Being and no-thingness emerge out of Tao as origin to find expression in different ways that complement one another. The last lines of chapter 11 sum it up well.

> Therefore in the being (*yu-chih*) of a thing,/ There lies the benefit (*li*).
> In the non-being (*wu-chih*) of a thing,/ there lies its use (*yun*).[49]

Being and non-being come together to represent and manifest Tao as function.[50]

As with this chapter of the *Tao Te Ching*, Heidegger's nothing is not a simple void, or an absence of things, but has a specific function. However, Heidegger takes one more step. The function of the nothing of the jug (which is holding) is complemented by the function of the clay vessel (which is pouring out). These two functions intersect in the jug's gift: the pouring out of the holding.

The active quality of the gift, the "pouring out of the holding," can be seen in other Heideggerian examples. In a general sense, when thing and nothing come together in balance (perhaps appropriately), a gift is created. The gift or work of the work of art might be seen in similar terms: a spilling out of what was once held. In another article Heidegger describes the work of persons in a similar manner:

> . . . man's existence is "held into" "this" nothingness, into this completely other of being. Put differently, this means, and could only mean, "Man is the seat-holder for nothingness." This sentence means that man is holding the place open for the complete other of being, so that in its openness there can be such a thing as being present (Being). Nothingness belongs . . . to being present.[51]

Persons may then be similar to Heidegger's jug. Just as the jug's gift is a "pouring out of the holding," so too with artwork and persons. The gift of persons (perhaps best seen in the poet) is also in the spilling out, or gushing forth, of the "holding" of nothingness.

But the later Heidegger may have a slightly different position on seeing, presence and nothing. In a poem entitled "Cézanne," originally published in 1971, Heidegger writes:

> In the later work of the painter, the duality
> of what is present and presence becomes one,
> "realized" and overcome at the same time,
> transformed into a mysterious identity.
> Is a path revealed here which would lead to
> a belonging together of poetry and thought?[52]

Heidegger mentions the gardener Vallier earlier in the poem, but does not specify a particular painting. Rather (as earlier with the reference to Van Gogh's paintings of shoes) he seems to be making a comment about the work of an artist at a particular point of time as evident in more than one painting. (In the last two years of his life Cézanne painted both water colour and oil portraits of the seated Vallier.)[53] Although we have no words of Heidegger here, the words of one art critic on Cézanne's last works seem to parallel those of Heidegger in the poem:

> The last watercolors have a gentler unity than those before. The correspondences of color melt together. The contained shadows in the tower of Saint Sauveur dissolve into the purple of the distance. The foliage and fruit of Cézanne's apple tree form a festive garland across the view over the town from his studio garden. The line is more tense and muscular then ever, but there is nevertheless a dissolution of the separateness of things and a total reconciliation of differences which often marks a great artist's last works.[54]

Cézanne's later paintings seem to have characteristics more usually associated with Monet and Impressionism than Van Gogh and Expressionism. It may be that the nature of Heidegger's nothing has changed; that it is no longer apart from things (frames things) but a part of things (somehow in things). In the Van Gogh painting, the nothing (the heavy black surrounding the shoe) served as boundary in the service of the thing: in the later Cézanne's work, the nothing is more in the thing, or put better, in things. In my reading and seeing, the move in Heidegger's choice of paintings from Van Gogh's shoes to the later Cézanne suggests a move from cising to non-cising in Heidegger's thinking. Although the one poem on a painting is not evidence enough of this in itself, it does offer some measure of visual support for the claim that a shift does take place (from cising to non-cising) in Heidegger's thinking and saying on nothing. The move is crucial for the link to a "Buddhism of presence" (developed at the end of this chapter). I think it is only at this point that Heidegger could say "things are empty."

2.3 Saying and Presence

In his later writings Heidegger turns from visual examples to language and poetry. One of the key writings here is the "Dialogue on language -- between a Japanese and an Inquirer," which originated in 1953/54.[55] In a representational sense the dialogue might be seen as an attempt to explore the question, If language is a "house of Being," is a conversation possible between two different "houses?" Or, Is there a common source of both houses that is somehow concealed? One of the pivotal points of the dialogue is the eventual utterance of *kotoba* as the Japanese word for language. But it is significant that this does not occur until page 45 of a 54 page dialogue.

Kotoba is only partially translated in the "Dialogue." *Ba* is translated as "leaves, including and especially the leaves of a blossom -- petals. Think of cherry blossoms or plum blossoms."[56] The difficulty rests with the translation of *koto*. Suggestions for a translation include "the breathlike advent of the stillness of delight,"[57] or "the happening of the lightening message of the graciousness that brings forth."[58] Language, or *kotoba*, is then "the petals that stem from *koto*."[59]

Steven Heine has pursued the Japanese context of kotoba more deeply. After connecting the *koto* (word) used in the dialogue with another *koto* (thing), he suggests *kotoba* is "part of a constellation of thing-word-mind whereby mind is continually perceiving and responding to things (*koto*) through poetic speech."[60] The creative oscillation of presencing would then take place in the gap between Heine's "perceiving and responding." However, Heine may have located too much agency in "mind." His statement might better reflect Heidegger's "attuning emptiness," or "that-which- regions" if it were reformulated just slightly: "mind is continually being created by and responding to things through poetic speech."

The word "emptiness" or (in Japanese) *kū* flows in and out of the dialogue on two earlier occasions (19, 41) and is linked to *kotoba* in its third appearance. Early in the conversation there is the equation of the Japanese emptiness and Being: "To us, emptiness is the loftiest name for what you mean to say with the word 'Being.'"[61] Later *kū* is introduced as the "sky's emptiness" which manifests "boundlessness." Heidegger then adds that "man" is "he who walks the boundary of the boundless." Finally *kū* enters the conversation concerning *kotoba*. The intersection and mutual interplay between *iro* (colour and sense) and *kū* (the open, emptiness) takes place through, and in, *koto*. It seems then (at least in my own reading of the "Dialogue") that *kotoba* may also be understood as *kūba* -- petals from emptiness.

It is at this point in the dialogue (when *kū* is linked to *kotoba*) that Heidegger introduces the term "saying" into the conversation. "Saying, then, is then not the name for human speaking . . . but for that essential being which your Japanese word *koto ba* hints and beckons. . . ."[63] Saying may then be close to a Heideggerian equivalent of *kotoba*.

Saying must be distinguished from speaking about. Heidegger comments:

> Speaking *about* language turns language almost inevitably into an object.
> . . . We then have taken up a position above language, instead of hearing
> from it.[64]

> ... Wherever the nature of language were to speak (say) to man as Saying,
> *it*, Saying, would bring about real dialogue ... which does not say "about"
> language but *of* language, as needfully used of its very nature.[65]

The difference between "saying" and "speaking about" seems to be similar to the difference between meditative and representational thought. Saying is an attempt at non-objectifying speaking.

In his later writings Heidegger continues to attempt to move from speaking about to saying. This is perhaps best seen in his use of Rilke's poetry in both a 1946 article "What are poets for?"[66] and in the 1964 letter to Stanley Romaine Hopper at Drew University.[67] When the fragments from Rilke used in the 1964 letter are combined, they read: "Song is existence . . . a breath for nothing."[68]

In the use of the first fragment, "song is existence," Heidegger states that "Song, the singing saying of the poet, is 'not coveting,' 'not soliciting,'. . . . Poetic saying is *Dasein*, Existence." Again, saying is a non-objectifying activity. It is not a "grasping or comprehending representation." The English word "comprehending" works very well here, signifying the kind of grasping understanding that is opposed to the non-attached openness Heidegger suggests.

In a later paragraph, Heidegger introduces a new fragment, "A breath for nothing." Breathing is an oscillating activity, a continual circle of taking in and letting go. But again the question of agency arises. In an earlier use of Rilke's poem, Heidegger seems to suggest that beings do not breathe but are breathed. One might say that in the same way word and nothing come together to create a poem, being and nothing come together to create a life. In this sense life or existence is, or can be, a poetic word . . . a word of song . . . a word that is sung in breath. The best of these breathings are sayings, thus "song is existence."

But Heidegger's letter includes a third fragment of Rilke's poem: ". . . " . Heidegger uses Rilke's ellipsis specifically: "Being in the presence of . . . ". These three dots, which Heidegger uses twice in the same way, suggest (or hint at) that which cannot be named, the *kū* that floats through the "Dialogue." Although Heidegger used Rilke's poem first in 1946, I think the letter of 1964 is an advance on this earlier work. In the earlier article Heidegger comments on Rilke's use of the three dots (". . . "). It might be said, then, that he "talks about" the three dots. In the Drew letter the three dots are not in quotation marks. It is Heidegger himself who uses the three dots, and he does so without explicitly pointing it out or discussing it. Again, the move is from "speaking about" (emptiness) to the expressive "saying" of ". . . ", a verbal equivalent of the visual move from cising to non-cising. Heidegger has become the poet of emptiness.

"Being in the presence of . . . "

The move from "speaking about" to "saying" in language seems to parallel a similar move in Heidegger's work with nothing. Heidegger's work with nothing goes through a number of overlapping phases: the metaphysical work on nothing; the distinction between nihilism and nothing; the visual approach to nothing; and finally, the relation between language and nothing.

Heidegger's early discussion of nothing can be seen in the 1929 "What is Metaphysics?"[69] where "nothing" is taken up as a metaphysical problem. Heidegger suggests that nothing can be approached in two ways: first, as negation, as "not"; and second, in a more fundamental way that precedes the use of nothing as "not." This second nothing can perhaps best be experienced within anxiety or dread (dread is different from fear, as fear has an object while dread does not).[70] Nothing here is somewhat threatening. It is a disruptive force. It creates a feeling of homelessness. Nothing functions mainly as contrast to sharpen that which is: one sees things against the nothing, or in comparison with the nothing.

Heidegger moves from this metaphysical discussion of nothing to a discussion of nothing in relation to nihilism. In Heidegger's last volume on Nietzsche (subtitled "Nihilism"), he attempts to place the question of nothing in historical context.[71] Nihilism is the result of a specific metaphysical framework (appearing at the end of the western metaphysical tradition) in which it is impossible to raise the question of the essence of nothing: nihilism is then the non-thinking of the essence of nothing. As David Krell puts it, destructive nihilism is the "non-essence of the nothing."[72]

In his later, more positive explorations of nothing Heidegger moves through "seeing" and "saying" (described above) to the fourfold -- a creative state formed by the intersection of mortals, gods, earth and sky. It is from the interplay of the fourfold that things emerge. It is the task of humans to step back from things and dwell in the fourfold. Heidegger articulates this position in "Building, Dwelling, Thinking" and "The Thing."[73] Both Being and Nothing are constituted by the intersecting of the fourfold. In a sense they are "crossed" by the fourfold and should be written as such: B̶e̶i̶n̶g̶, N̶o̶t̶h̶i̶n̶g̶.[74] Heidegger states:

> Nothingness would have to be written, and that means thought of, just like B̶e̶i̶n̶g̶. . . . The essence of man itself belongs to the essence of nihilism and thereby to the phase of its completion. Man, as the essence put into use in B̶e̶i̶n̶g̶ helps to constitute the zone of B̶e̶i̶n̶g̶ and that means at the same time of nothingness. Man does not only stand in the critical zone of the line. He himself, but not he for himself and particularly not through himself alone, is this zone and thus the line.[75]

Persons are this critical zone of the line, the zone of the "crossed" nothingness.

This, I think, is a change from the nature of the nothing in "What is metaphysics?" The abyss between Being and beings has turned into the home of nothingness. Whereas the early nothings seem to have a dark or heavy quality to them (dread, abyss, homelessness), the later, poetic nothings are lighter in both senses of the word. Although this could be read as a change in positions, it could also be read as a shift in emphasis from one aspect of the nothing to the other: an exploration of the different nuances of the original nothing as they were revealed to Heidegger's changing thinking. The recoil of nothing seems to have had an effect. When the "homelessness" of nothing in 1929 becomes more of a "home" of nothing in the 1950's, perhaps it is not nothing that has changed, but Heidegger.

2.4 Presencing and Ethics

Thus far, Heideggerian thinking seems quite plausible as a mode of responding to the world, but the question remains as to whether or not there is a basis for decision-making in this thought. What are the consequences of choosing this particular working of emptiness to guide action?   How might this particular working of emptiness structure the thinking used to make decisions?

Let me first try to outline Heidegger's position before pursuing these difficult questions. Perhaps the best place to begin is with the question put to Heidegger by Jean Beaufret shortly after World War II: "When are you going to write an ethics?" An exploration of Heidegger's answer to that query, the 1947 "Letter on Humanism" helps situate the relationship between the working of nothing (or emptiness) and ethics.[76]

Heidegger's response suggests Beaufret's question missed the mark. An ethics in the traditional sense, a set of rules, or a code of conduct, assumes the very rational ground in humankind that Heidegger wishes to question. Heidegger's project takes a step back from such rules (and the logical thinking they presuppose) and inquires as to origins. On what ground can such rules exist?

But there may be another sense of "ethics," an ethics which could rather be thought in terms of *ethos*. Heidegger writes:

> If the name "ethics," in keeping with the basic meaning of the word *ethos*, should now say that "ethics" ponders the abode of man, then that thinking which thinks the truth of Being as the primordial element of man, as one who eksists, is in itself the original ethics. However, this thinking is not ethics in the first instance, because it is ontology.[77]

This second sense of ethics requires a mode of thinking other than logic. Heidegger suggests that this kind of ethics will require the kind of thinking outlined earlier in this chapter as meditative thinking. He recognizes, however, that this has not answered the question of ethics, only relocated it. "Whence does thinking take its measure? What law governs its deeds?"[78]

Heidegger provides only general hints on the form such a "law" might take. "The fittingness of the saying of Being, as of the destiny of truth, is the first law of thinking."[79] Thinking might be measured by "rigor of meditation, carefulness in saying, frugality with words."[80] The letter ends with the original question displaced, but still largely unanswered. Perhaps from Heidegger's perspective it must remain so. As Schurmann puts it, Beaufret's mistake was to think that "the phenomenological *traits* of praxis could somehow be converted into *norms*, or descriptive categories into prescriptive ones."[81]

But perhaps Heidegger's thinking on ethics can be pushed further than he took it himself. Upon what "edge" might an "ethic of presencing" be based?

Presencing has its origins in the tension created between world and thing as they alternate between revealing and concealing. It is by attention to boundary, border, edge, difference that we let the artwork/thing work, and subject/object duality collapses (or is simply not created). The danger here is that presencing can be turned into an aesthetic experience. This happens when the play of the artwork is fixed: Being is then turned into a being and the artwork into a thing. The work of the artwork (which is the play) "opens up a world and keeps it abidingly in force."[82] It is this play that keeps thinking opening and which an aesthetic experience closes. Presencing, then, rests upon a maintenance of the play that is possible when one highlights boundary/difference.

The wish to maintain presencing could well be used as a basis for decision-making. Actions consistent with presencing would then be considered "ethical." Actions that required the abandonment of the activity of presencing would then be "unethical." This sense of "ethics" is close to Heidegger's suggestion that ethics be rethought as "ethos." A being is at home in the oscillation of presencing. An ethical action is then one that is in harmony with the work of emptiness as presence or presencing.

Heideggerian presencing seems to have both a synchronic and a diachronic movement. Synchronically, presencing is the oscillation of the going-in and coming-out in any given moment, the maintenance of the state of opening. However, diachronically, presencing may be progressive: it seems to me that there is both the becoming black of being and the becoming light of nothingness. There is an "edge" in any given moment of presencing, and when these moments are connected, the "edge" can be seen to move. Presencing increases both qualitatively and quantitatively. The long term practice of presencing then results in the greater frequency of a increasing sense of lighting, opening, and clearing. In my reading, this is suggested by parallel movements (from cising to non-cising) in Heidegger's thinking, saying and seeing. It is through engaging in the act of presencing that one is "attuned" by the "attuning emptiness." I think that it is in this two-fold sense that practice of presencing could guide decision-making. As we shall see, however, there is a serious flaw in this "ethics of presencing."

2.5 Heidegger, Presence and Buddhism

> In 1938 [Keiji] Nishitani was doing research in Freiburg, where Heidegger was teaching, and ordered from Blackwells in England the first volume of [D.T.] Suzuki's *Essays in Zen Buddhism*, which he presented to Heidegger for his birthday. Shortly thereafter, Heidegger sent a card inviting Nishitani to visit him at his home; it turned out that he had already read Suzuki's book and was eager to discuss it.[83]

> If I understand this man [D.T. Suzuki] correctly, this is what I have been trying to say in all my writings.[84]
>
> - Heidegger

This chapter has drawn on Heidegger's writings to present one reading of the work of emptiness. Although I have used "presence" or "presencing" as the umbrella term to describe the particular nature of this work of emptiness, a number of other Heideggerian terms or phrases could have been chosen: two obvious possibilities are "releasement" (*Gelassenheit*) and "meditative thinking," both of which are used above in the development of presencing. I see these three activities of presencing, releasement and meditative thinking as roughly equivalent in Heidegger.

There are many scholars who read Buddhism in a way that seems quite compatible with Heidegger and presencing. Although such a reading of Buddhism does not require explicit use of, or comparison with Heidegger's writings, many scholars have found Heidegger's thought very useful in attempts to work out and present their positions on Buddhism. Within Buddhism itself, many of the members of one stream of Japanese Buddhist philosophy, the Kyoto school, have been heavily influenced by their study of (and in some cases with) Heidegger. Indeed, Yasuo Yuasa has commented that "there is probably general agreement that among philosophers in the contemporary world Heidegger has left the greatest as well as the most continuous influence on philosophy in Japan."[85] The inclusion of this section on "Buddhism and Presence" emphasizes, again, that this chapter (or chapters three or four) is not just an investigation of a particular thinker; rather it is an exploration of a particular working of emptiness that may be common to a number of different thinkers, both "West" and "East."

Presencing, releasement and/or meditative thinking figure prominently in the work of scholars who use the comparison with Heidegger directly in their presentation of Buddhism. Joan Stambaugh, who has had a long career as a translator and interpreter of Heidegger, is a good example. In her text on Dōgen, *Impermanence is Buddha-nature: Dōgen's Understanding of Temporality*,[86] she equates releasement (*Gelassenheit*) with Dōgen's "dropping off of body and mind."[87] Her concluding chapter is a very careful development of thinking in Dōgen and Heidegger (in which Heidegger is footnoted ten times), based on Heidegger's two kinds of thinking. The basic thesis of her position might be summed up in the following statement:

> There is a remarkable affinity between Heidegger's representational and calculative thinking and Dōgen's ordinary, discriminating mind (*citta*), and between Heidegger's meditative thinking and Dōgen's Buddha-mind.[88]

It is important to note that the equation here is not between Heidegger's meditative thinking and Dōgen's meditative thinking, but between Heidegger's meditative thinking and Dōgen's "Buddha-mind." Stambaugh's reading of Dōgen rests upon the position that the practice of Buddhist meditation literally is enlightenment; and that this meditation/enlightenment is basically a synchronic process where any diachronic movement is limited to some sort of deepening of the synchronic process. It is this position that, in my mind, unifies a number of different thinkers under the heading "Buddhism and presence" (e.g. T.P. Kasulis, David Shaner, Michael Zimmerman, Francis Cook, Masao Abe, Christopher Ives and Joan Stambaugh).[89]

Of the group of scholars who read Buddhism in general, and Dōgen in particular, in this manner, Francis Cook presents one of the most comprehensive positions. Cook uses Heidegger's concepts of "inauthentic" and "authentic" to describe the difference between the ordinary (deluded) state of mind and enlightenment in Dōgen. Cook's inauthentic self results from an anxiety-produced thinking which sees the self and things as separate. Authentic selfhood "results from the restoration of original unity."[90] Cook writes:

> In terms used in [Dōgen's] "Genjōkōan," when the self in its assumed

separateness imposes subjective meaning on experience, inauthenticity results ("Conveying the self to the myriad things to authenticate them is delusion"). On the other hand, when the self is made authentic by experience (the myriad things) or is made a self by them, the result is authentic selfhood. In this matter, Heidegger says something similar about authenticity. According to Michael Zimmerman, Heidegger's lifelong search for authenticity disclosed that the authentic self is not revealed when one engages in theoretical self-reflection but rather is disclosed "in the worldly things with whom I concern myself."[91]

Cook's emphasis on dissolving the subject-object split and developing a thinking other than "theoretical self-reflection" is quite compatible with the working of emptiness as presence or presencing. Cook goes on to suggest that this switch from the inauthentic to the authentic can be used to understand the experience of enlightenment in Dōgen (Dōgen's "dropping off of body and mind").

Although Stambaugh and Cook differ slightly in their presentations of Heidegger and Dōgen, these differences are far less important than their agreement on the essential issue: the unity of Buddhist practice and enlightenment within a certain kind of thinking (or nonthinking) described in this chapter as "presencing."[92] The extreme claim would be this: Heideggerian presencing is Buddhist enlightenment. Or, as Zimmerman puts it, "What Buddhism speaks of as enlightenment, or liberation from the craving for things, Heidegger speaks of as *Gelassenheit*, releasement from the will to power over all things."[93] While scholars of a "Buddhism of presencing" place one or two (minor) restrictions on the comparison between Heidegger and Dōgen (Heidegger's thinking does not extend to nature,[94] it cannot be extended to scientific thought,[95] and it is concerned with historical periods[96]), the main problem is never with the fundamental nature of Heideggerian thinking.

2.6 Presencing and Co-dependent Arising

In any "Buddhism of presencing," the implications of thinking as presencing must be extended to embrace all things. The presencing of the self is intimately linked to the presencing of others: the emptiness of the self is simultaneously the emptiness of others. This is the theoretical move that links meditative thinking to the affirmative reading of (co)dependent arising. Francis Cook, for example, extends his concept of "authenticity" to an "absolute nothingness" of all things. "The actualization of the self as absolute nothingness (*zettai mu*), which I have been calling 'authentic selfhood,' is simultaneously the realization that everything else without exception is also this same absolute nothingness."[97]

Christopher Ives, in a similar reading of Buddhism, puts this double aspect of the work of emptiness very well in referring to soteriological and metaphysical notions of emptiness (*śūnyatā*). Ives notes:

> As a logical and metaphysical term, *śūnyatā* indicates both the lack of any independent essence or self in things and the interrelational dynamism that constitutes things. As a soteriological notion, *śūnyatā* signifies the elimination of suffering (Sanskrit, *duhkha*) that arises when people posit themselves as independent "selves" over against independent "things" and through this fixation sever themselves from the world and cling to objects or conditions . . . [98]

Presencing (*śūnyata* as a soteriological notion), is thus linked to co-dependent arising (*śūnyatā* as a metaphysical notion). The emptiness of thinking and concepts is extended to people and things: the internal position becomes an external one. Internally, emptiness functions to end suffering and clinging. There is a shift from attachment to non-attachment through a specific practice of thinking understood here as the "presencing" of all that is. Externally, this "presencing" results in an understanding of the "interrelationality" of all things that is one reading of co-dependent arising.

These internal and external perspectives are illuminated in the image of Indra's Net, a net of infinite proportions with jewels at each of the joins. One scholar describes Indra's Net as follows:

> Far away in the heavenly abode of the great god Indra, there is a wonderful net that has been hung. . . in such a manner that it stretches out infinitely in all directions. . . . [A] single glittering jewel hangs in each "eye" of the net, and since the net itself is infinite in all dimensions, the jewels are infinite in number. . . . If we now arbitrarily select one of the jewels for inspection, and look closely at it, we will discover that in its polished surface there are reflected all other jewels in the net, infinite in number. Not only that, but each of the jewels reflected in this one jewel is also reflecting all the other jewels, so that there is an infinite reflecting process occurring.[99]

Each jewel is thus positioned to reflect and be reflected in all the others. When one is able to practice non-attachment, one then authenticates one's original nature reflecting and being reflected in all other jewels.

The dominant understanding of Buddhist emptiness as a whole, as well as Dōgen's emptiness in particular, seems to be through this affirmative reading of co-dependent arising. For example, Shohei Ichimura states that:

> . . . Dōgen's dialectical thinking . . . can best be analyzed and comprehended on the basis of the "dialectical context" out of which Nāgārjuna and his followers justified the Mādhyamika approach. It is my contention that Buddhist thinkers, whether of Indian, Chinese, or Japanese origin, have invariably made such a dialectical context the basis of their insight into and demonstration of *śūnyatā*, and hence that it is this dialectical context that transcends every and any form of cultural and linguistic heritage.[100]

Ichimura uses Nāgārjuna's example of the co-dependency of "light" and "dark" to illustrate this dialectical context. As Ichimura puts it, though "light" and "dark" are "conceptually incompatible, [they] are in convention required to be co-present."[101] The two concepts are dependent on one another for their existence, yet not the same. They are "simultaneously different and yet identical."[102] Since they have no individual existence, they are "empty." They are simultaneously "existent" and "non-existent."[103] Again, this is the affirmative logic of "is/is not" where all things are simultaneously negated and affirmed.

Francis Cook also advocates such a position in a paper entitled "Just This: Buddhist Ultimate Reality," an excellent summary of the affirmative "co-dependent arising is primary" position. Cook states:

> . . . when I search for something that most, perhaps all, Buddhists from the primitive Buddhism of the first centuries to the Buddhism of Keiji Nishitani would accept as ultimate, I am led to *śūnyatā* and its synonym, *pratītya-samutpāda* [(co)-dependent arising]. That is to say, despite significant cultural variations in world Buddhism, all forms would agree that if there is a reality, existence, or being, beyond which it is futile to seek, and thus is the end, it is the world itself as the place where everything exists as the result of everything else in a vast inconceivable web of mutual conditioning. . . . Whatever Buddhists may actually believe, and whatever mythological or figurative language they may employ in talking about ultimate reality, they <u>ought to</u> finally mean *pratītya-samutpāda*.[104]

There is a three-part argument: first *śūnyatā* is the ultimate; second, *śūnyatā* and *pratītya-samutpāda* are literally synonymous; and (therefore) third, *pratītya-samutpāda* is ultimate reality.

But there is a serious ethical problem here. Although in theory co-dependent arising is the basis for a Buddhist ethic of "relationality" or "reciprocity," in practice this has proved to be no barrier to putting "pure experience" to use towards any end. The wish to cultivate and maintain presencing can govern decision-making in daily life, but this choice seems independent of (rather than co-dependent with) whatever external objects or conditions are being "presenced."

In other words, while one can assert that there is a link between presencing and co-dependent arising, and choose to act as if there were such a link, it is not <u>necessary</u> to link the two. The internal act of presencing is not dependent upon behaviour that acknowledges the co-dependence of external things -- the two can be mutually exclusive. There is no "edge" in presencing requiring a change in the nature of external <u>or</u> internal conditions. Presencing is a neutral skill which, theoretically, should improve one's ability to do absolutely anything. The "Zen" samurai may be seen as a governing example. Where is the ethical edge in presencing if he can dwell in "no-mind" and lop off the head of his enemy? Critics point to the historical use of Zen Buddhism by both business and the military in articles such as "Japanese Corporate Zen" and "The Zen of Japanese Nationalism." Among the points made in these articles: that Zen practice is seen to offer great "benefits" to those interested in pursuing careers in corporations and the military; that there has been a long identification of Buddhism with the welfare of the Emperor and the interests of the Japanese nation; and that Buddhist scriptures and meditative techniques have often been put to use in the service of feudal lords.[105]

The title of a recent article by Paul Swanson "'Zen is not Buddhism,'" sums up the extreme position: "Zen is not Buddhism" because there is no critical or ethical edge. The "Zen" referred to here seems to be that of D.T. Suzuki and the Kyoto School (both are mentioned in the article).[106] If so, then the working of emptiness in this "Zen" (of "Zen is not Buddhism") would be very similar to that of the "Buddhism of presencing" presented in this chapter. Clearly, this movement will add even greater weight to the ethical pressure now being put on Buddhist/Zen emptiness.

The link to Heidegger is also highly problematic for any Buddhist ethic based on "presencing." Recent scholarship documenting Heidegger's involvement with Nazism has raised serious ethical questions about the fundamental nature of Heideggerian thinking. Let me repeat the charge directed at Heidegger's thinking in the introduction: there is nothing in the structure of Heidegger's thinking to prevent the slide into Nazism.[107] To my knowledge, not one of the scholars who has appropriated Heidegger's work (directly or indirectly) in his or her philosophical interpretation of Buddhist practice has addressed the ethical issues that appropriation now raises. The "Buddhism of presencing" seems not only vulnerable to charges against Heidegger but to an additional one as well: what about "internal Nazis?" How does one account fully for the doctrine of karma and the vast literature on "hindrances" or "defilements" in Buddhism? Are these "presenced" as well?

But do the second or third readings of emptiness offer a compelling alternative? Do they work a different "edge" in emptiness? Let me carry these questions forward to the workings of emptiness (and the accompanying alternate readings of Buddhism) presented in the following chapters.

3 THE WORKING OF DIFFERENCE: MARK C. TAYLOR, DIFFERENCE AND DEPENDENT ARISING

But what has theology not thought? . . . Different philosophical and theological positions represent contrasting accounts of the original ground from which everything emerges and to which (the) all returns. . . . In thinking the being of beings, ontotheology leaves nothing unthought. This claim must be understood in at least two ways. In the first place, originary thinking seeks to be comprehensive. . . . In the second place, ontotheology leaves nothing unthought by not thinking nothing.

-- Mark C. Taylor[108]

Nāgārjuna's attack on the entitative theory of existence (*bhāva*) by means of the notion of emptiness (*śūnyatā*) closely resembles Derrida's criticism of the principle of identity through the notion of *différance*. Furthermore, if viewed in terms of "co-dependent origination" (*pratītya-samutpāda*), *śūnyatā* approaches the "non-original origin" that I have reinterpreted in terms of the divine milieu.

-- Mark C. Taylor[109]

What is the nature of the "original ground from which everything emerges and to which (the) all returns?" What is prior to thought? For Mark Taylor, something is necessary for thought or image to come into being, and that something is a line of difference -- a nothing. This line of difference/nothing <u>precedes</u> the specificity of whatever is being distinguished and thus precedes all opposites. For Taylor, the "play" is the play of a neutral mean which now divides and now joins. This neutral mean, or difference, is Taylor's non-dual "Holy Nothing" which makes all things possible with its presence/absence. While both Heidegger and Taylor are committed to the maintenance of a certain "play of nothing," the components of this play appear to be different.

These two positions on play are evident in "Paralectics," where Taylor reads Gadamer against Derrida.[110] I see Gadamer's view as similar to the position of

Heidegger presented in chapter two, while Derrida's position is close to that of Mark Taylor.[111] In making his point, Taylor comments on the transformative power of the play in dialogue in Gadamer's *Truth and Method*. He states:

> When dialogue becomes "a communion, in which we do not remain what we were," conversation is truly edifying. Edifying discourse involves a sharing that unites rather than divides, joins rather than separates.[112]

In this "educational model" of dialogue we each learn from the differences of the other and become something more than we were. An attempt is made to expand thinking, incorporate differences and come to some common understanding.

However, Taylor suggests that the "play of dialogue" can be thought differently. "Suppose play does not issue in presence or representation but stages their impossibility."[113] He writes:

> While dialectical (i.e. hermeneutical) dialogue is either deaf to, or tries to silence, every such difference, non-dialectical dialogue solicits an other it can neither contain nor express.[114]

And later in the article:

> As that which never ends, the "beginning" of the neuter is the "before" of play -- the before that is forever "before the alternative of presence and absence." A dialogue that does not incorporate difference and appropriate the other by becoming dialectical must repeatedly "speak" the outlines of the between.[115]

This neuter/between/other is Taylor's "nothing."

I see a significant difference here between Taylor and Heidegger. In Heidegger the play of nothing is in the service of, or is itself, a unifying poetic non-duality while in Taylor the play of a different nothing is an irreparable tear. In Heidegger that which guides decision-making is the wish to maintain a poetic mode of presencing while in Taylor it is the recognition of the edge/rift/tear/difference which must not (or rather cannot) ever be suppressed.

3.1 Drawing Difference

> Though the meaning of "drawing" is undecidable, its oscillation and alternation involve a rhythm that suggests the "origin of the work of art." ...As a rend(er)ing that simultaneously opens and closes, drawing marks and remarks the opening or clearing in which figures appear and disappear.[116]

One draws not only in making lines with a pencil but also in pulling cards from a deck or water from a well. In other senses of draw, a group of soldiers may draw up in front of a reviewing stand when they assume a specific order or arrangement; or, in billiards, one may draw the cue ball back by using backspin. How, and in which order, does Taylor's thinking draw up? What kind of spin is involved in Taylor's thinking? To draw is also to make metal into wire by pulling it through holes. Clearly the nature of the holes will determine the final shape of the wire. What kind of holes, or nothings, does Taylor draw through in his thinking? In relation to the present project, one might ask "How and what does Taylor's mode of thinking draw forth when it creates and selects in visually organizing and representing a personal reality? How does Taylor's thinking spin, shape, pull and order . . . and through which kind of holes?"

Taylor's drawing of "difference" needs to be examined in two steps. The first step in exploring Taylor's drawing involves the last section of the 1982 text *Deconstructing Theology*, "Tracing," where Taylor experiments with figure-ground drawing. Under a heading "Optical Allusions: Hieroglyphics as Hierophany," Taylor reproduces the classic gestalt faces/goblet image (see Figure 1).

Figure 1: Faces/Goblet Image

Underneath the image Taylor writes:

> Ground grounds figure -- figure turns from and returns to ground. Only
> so is figure ground-ed. Yet a figureless ground is groundless. Ground,
> therefore, is figural. Figure grounds ground. Figure(s) ground(s) figure(s)
> ground(s) figure(s) ground(s). . . . [118]

Taylor introduces the possibility here that the figure may be approached in such a way that neither image predominates. The images are interdependent. As neither one can exist without the other it would be a mistake to privilege either one. As we shall see, this way of drawing is both similar to yet slightly different from Heidegger.

Another part from the same section helps highlight this difference with Heidegger. In a new typeface with additional space between all letters Taylor writes:

> White space is the emptiness which surrounds
> and invades the word. Without white space, there
> is only darkness, invisibility. Black space is
> the fullness which surrounds and invades the
> wordless. Without dark space, there is only
> light, invisibility. Word reveals the fullness of
> emptiness and the emptiness of fullness. Writing
> is scripture, the play, or the interplay of white
> space and black space which enlightens by
> bringing darkness to light and light to darkness.
> Words or Golgotha. [119]

Taylor articulates a view of complete interdependence. For Taylor (in this 1982 text) there is a play between word and nothing, silence and speech, light and dark, with neither one dominant. Emptiness is now an interdependent opposite of fullness with both playing back and forth as equal partners.

A second step in examining Taylor's thinking/drawing involves a look at the slightly different concept of nothing in the 1987-90 works *Altarity* and *Tears*.[120] In *Tears,* the image Taylor uses to represent his nothing at play is quite different from the faces/goblet figure. The first figure in *Tears* is a picture of Enrique Espinosa's sculptural work "The Silence of Jesus." Rather than attempt to represent Jesus in a traditional manner as a positive presence, Espinosa has taken the opposite tack and "frames" Jesus as an "absence."

The faces/goblet image can help explain Espinosa's work. It would be possible to cut two black surfaces and bring them together side by side to create a "goblet" space in the faces/goblet image. The "goblet" would then be represented not as a positive white surface, but as the space between the carved edges of the two black surfaces. Similarly, Espinosa uses the carved edges of two black plates to create an image of Jesus (or rather, an absence of Jesus). There is "nothing" between the two black plates. Jesus is now "nothing."

Taylor's use of Espinosa suggests that the "sacred" nothing is now not an interdependent opposite, but a gap or crack. While the gap, fissure, crack, is still dependent on forms, it is no longer an opposite but a neutral or mean. This is a crucial difference: nothing or emptiness has shifted from an opposite (of fullness) to a non-dual neuter. It is now neither the emptiness nor the fullness (nor their interdependence) that is drawn, but the edge, border, rim, gap between the two.

But my use of the Espinosa piece is slightly misleading. Care must be taken to combat the tendency to objectify the "edge/gap" by giving it substance. This tendency may be especially strong during the consideration of what Taylor draws from art. Although the physical space between the two forms in the Espinosa work can be given solidity as negative space -- Jesus reified as nothing -- this is not Taylor's intention. Any figure-ground reading of Taylor's difference must be backed up at least one more step: Taylor's difference is not the ground between two figures but the edge/crack/gap which distinguishes figure and ground. And if that difference is substantialized and drawn forth then Taylor's edge/crack/difference must slip away again. By definition, the spatiality of Taylor's difference forever eludes one's grasp.

It is this rim, border, cut that creates difference and thus even precedes the distinction between emptiness and fullness. It is an edge/difference that "cleaves" together and apart, and therefore plays between joining and separating. Taylor writes:

> "Cleave" means not only divide, separate, split and fissure, but also adhere, stick and cling. Cleaving, therefore, simultaneously divides and joins. This joint is the hinge upon which "the Origin of the Work of Art" swings.[121]

The play that precedes presence and absence is this out-line which both joins and separates. The work of this nothing makes both similarity and difference possible. Because it precedes presence and absence it is also prior to thought.

Clearly one cannot think what is prior to thought. However, the difference that is prior to thought does play in and out of what <u>is</u> present in thought in such a way that complete presence is always disrupted. As Taylor states: "Consciousness, therefore, is always incomplete, and transparent self-consciousness forever impossible."[122]

If we now compare the Taylor in step one and step two we can see that there has been a move from the non-privileging of interdependent opposites (figure/ground) to the drawing of a neutral mean. Although the nature of visual cutting or cising has not changed, drawing has changed. Taylor now draws a non-dual nothing, a nothing that no longer exists interdependently and that must always slip away.

3.2 Taylor's Critique of the Logic of Presence: Thomas J.J. Altizer

> The heart of modernism is, in Shattuck's phrase, a profound longing for "a full aliveness to the present moment." The aim of diverse modernist practices in art, architecture, and theology is the enjoyment of "total presence" *here and now*.[123]

Taylor's postmodern position on the work of difference, and its expression in art, becomes clearer when seen in contrast with Thomas J. J. Altizer's position on "total presence."[124] Altizer's lifelong project, a radical re-reading of Christianity, has been heavily influenced by his study of Mahāyāna Buddhism. Altizer's Buddhist-inspired postmodern theology might be summed up as follows:

i. The death of God is an emptying activity in which the transcendent becomes immanent.

ii. This emptying process results in a "total presence" in the actual now, which is already taking place. (To put it another way, "total presence" is the work of emptying or emptiness.)

iii. This emptying process is an historical movement which will reach its culmination in an apocalyptic moment.[125]

Mark Taylor's critique of Altizer can also be summed up in three points:[126]

i. There is a consistent desire for presence in Altizer's choice of language, in the consistent use of terms such as "origins," "source," "ground," and "identity." However, from Taylor's perspective, any desire for presence implies lack, therefore presence is not primary (and an "origin") but must be secondary. If anything is "primary" it must be difference.

ii. Altizer's use of the "logic of negation" has a positive reserve. In other words, the effect of Altizer's negative dialectic is not negative but positive. It is actually a process of affirmation (which in the end yields total presence). Negation itself is negated in an attempt to cover over the lack. "The negation of negation issues in a total affirmation that overcomes every trace of unreconciled otherness."[127] However, from Taylor's perspective (as he has pointed out in *Erring* and elsewhere), the deferral of *différance* means that lack is a "wound" that is primary rather than secondary and thus can never be "healed."

iii. This gap, wound or difference is a negative that cannot be negated. It is unknowable, in that it forever eludes our grasp. It is forever deferred and <u>cannot</u> be brought to presence. As Taylor has put it:

By declaring the death of God, Altizer does not call into question the traditional understanding of Being in terms of presence. To the contrary, he insists that to be is to be present, and to be fully is to be present totally. Although never stated in these terms, Altizer's argument implies that the mistake of classical theism . . . is not that it misunderstands Being as such, but that it identifies the locus of true Being as transcendent to, rather than immanent in, the world of space and time.[128]

In contrast to this, Taylor sees the task of the theologian differently: "how to think otherwise than being by thinking a difference that is not reducible to identity."[129]

Taylor uses the visual realm to illustrate his critique of Altizer and presence. Selected paintings represent different views of the work of nothing or emptiness. However, the selection of art and how it is read may well be dependent on the nature of the "self" one brings to it. There is a reciprocal exchange between the viewer and the painting, and "total presence" (or not) occurs in this exchange. As Taylor states: "the work of art is not to reconcile opposites but to articulate differences."[130] However, which differences are articulated may depend on which naught is (not) being thought. In this sense the selection and reading of a painting acts like a mirror, adding to and reflecting back the nature of one's own experience of the self and the working of nothing.

In a 1990 article Taylor contrasts the modernist wish to represent "total presence," which he sees in the monochromatic paintings of Yves Klein, with the postmodern position that total presence is impossible, which he sees in the "gappy" paintings of Lucio Fontana.[131] The Klein painting, an intense blue monochrome, represents the "no thing that is in all things," a "painterly vision of classical negative theology," and the "unitive ecstasy with the all."[132] As Taylor sums up his reading of Klein's painting: "the apocalyptic fire of blue consumes everything by returning all things to the no thing of the void in which emptiness is fullness."[133]

The work of Lucio Fontana, however, represents (to Taylor) quite a different view of "nothing." These works are characterized by a series of "cuts" or "tears" in a monochromatic canvas (see Figure 2).

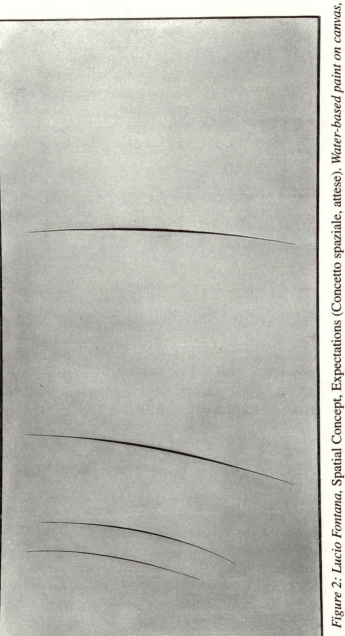

Figure 2: Lucio Fontana, Spatial Concept, Expectations (Concetto spaziale, attese). Water-based paint on canvas, 1959, 126 x 250.9 cm. (Solomon R. Guggenheim Museum, New York, Gift, Mrs. Teresita Fontana, Milan, 1977. Photograph by Robert E. Mates © The Solomon R. Guggenheim Foundation, New York.)

Taylor comments on the Fontana piece as follows:

> The tear in the canvas interrupts the plenitude of the formless void by creating an opening to a "beyond" that is (impossibly) both inside and outside the painted surface. . . . Rather than the no thing that is in all things, Fontana's nothing implies a lack of being that neither exists nor does not exist. The lack is (not) the absence of the frame but repeatedly remarks the frame "within" the work itself, thereby reinscribing precisely the margin of difference that Klein, like all modernists, struggles to erase or efface.[134]

Again, this "difference" or "margin of difference" is the central concept in Taylor's work, yet even phrasing it in these terms is problematic. To understand difference as a concept is to risk turning it into a tool, technique, or object. It would be more accurate to say that difference in Taylor is a (non)concept or an (un)thought.[135]

3.3 Presence, Difference and Dependent Arising

> I wonder if deconstruction is truly so easy in Japan. I have my doubts about whether we can say that deconstruction is a direct element in Japanese-type thought. Certainly, Japanese often say that Buddhist thought or the Zen of Dōgen was already a kind of deconstruction, but I wonder if that is so.
>
> -- Jacques Derrida[136]

> Though initially the "middle way" of Buddhism seems analogous to the neither/nor of the not, Nishitani's effort to reconcile East and West exposes a metaphysics of being implicit in his doctrine of nothingness. Rather than a world-negating nihilism, Nishitani's religion of nothingness ends in an affirmation of the world that leaves no space for the critical resistance necessary for ethical action.
>
> -- Mark C. Taylor[137]

Given Taylor's reading of "emptiness and presence" in Altizer, one might expect him to be equally critical of any reading of "nothingness and presence" in Buddhism. Indeed, Taylor indicts the attempt to "recover presence" or "heal the wound" in the work of Keiji Nishitani of the Kyoto school.

Let me (briefly) present Nishitani's position before turning to Taylor's critique. Although his language is slightly different, Nishitani's work is dependent on a working of emptiness (or nothingness) that is close to the two-part understanding of emptiness presented in the Buddhism section of the previous chapter: first, emptiness is realized in a certain type of thinking (similar to Heidegger's presencing, releasement, or meditative thought); second, this thinking reveals the true nature and relationship of all things (all things are interdependent in their emptiness). In a section on the meditation practice of Dōgen's Zen, Nishitani writes:

> The point of absolute nonobjectifiability -- where the eye does not see the eye, the fire does not burn fire . . . and yet, for this very reason, where the eye sees things, the fire burns things . . . is a point that withdraws beyond all reason and *logos* and can only open up in the Existenz of the dropping off of body and mind. Where fire, as something that does not burn itself, is fire (or is in the mode of being of fire) . . . is what I have called "samadhi-being" or "position." This is the nonobjectifiable mode of being of a thing as it is in itself.[138]

This is the "is/is not" (or "is not/is") logic that characterizes the Kyoto school. It is through negation (or a series of negations) that "things" come into being on their own home-ground: the "field of nihility" is negated and becomes the affirming "field of emptiness."

Nishitani makes the same point slightly differently in developing a statement of Dōgen's on observance, zazen and "self-joyous samadhi." Nishitani writes:

> . . . observance means the samadhi of self-enjoyment, an absolute freedom of harmony or Order. . . . we have no cause to inflict a wound on this Order by letting an act of reflective thought intervene . . . . No sooner has the attitude of objective representation come on the scene than "Form" as something outside the self, is generated. . . .One has already deviated from observance.[139]

This "absolute freedom of harmony or Order" made possible by "nonobjectifiability" is Nishitani's field of emptiness.

Altizer's connection to the Kyoto school becomes interesting at this point. Altizer's view that "total presence" results from the work of emptiness leads him to draw emptiness or nothingness with a "logic of presence" and this extends to his reading of Buddhism. His articles rely on the dialectical logic of negation, but in a way that necessarily stresses affirmation rather than deferral. Again, this is the key point of difference between Altizer and Taylor as well as between the two readings of Buddhism with which they seem to connect. Altizer's affirmative use of negation and his reading of emptiness or nothingness as "presence" resonates somewhat with the Kyoto school's affirmative use of the logic of "is/is not" and "Absolute Nothingness." This has allowed Altizer to take part in a conversation with this strain of Buddhist thought. Altizer has articles in recent volumes on both Keiji Nishitani (1989) and Masao Abe (1990).[140]

In his critique of Nishitani, Taylor makes two points that echo his critique of Altizer.[141] First, Taylor states that Nishitani's "commitment to something like ontotheology" can be seen in his use of categories such as "ground," "home-ground," "primal fact," "things as they are in themselves" and "All are one."[142] Second, Nishitani's philosophy ends in a "recovery of unity through an absolute negation that is an absolute affirmation."[143] Taylor ends his article with a third point directed at Nishitani's statement that the field of *śūnyatā* is a field of force:

> Force, therefore, is never simply one but is always already divided between forces. This between is not a home-ground that serves as a secure base or faultless foundation. . . .The not of the play of forces is more unsettling than the negation of negation, for it calls forth resistance. . . . There is nothing elemental about the not, for nothing is elemental. Nor is this "no play" primal, for nothing is primal. If, however, nothing is elemental, if nothing is primal, then there is no home-ground. In the absence of a home-ground, any return to the all is impossible.

But I have suggested that not all readings of Buddhism may contain this element of affirmation. Indeed, Taylor himself has suggested (at least twice) that there may well be strong parallels between Nāgārjuna's (co)dependent arising and Derrida's *différance*. He footnotes Nāgārjuna when discussing "origination" in *Erring*,[144] but his strongest comment comes in a published response to a panel review of this book. Taylor states:

> Nāgārjuna's attack on the entitative theory of existence (*bhāva*) by means of the notion of emptiness (*śūnyatā*) closely resembles Derrida's criticism of the principle of identity through the notion of *différance*. Furthermore, if viewed in terms of "co-dependent origination" (*pratītya-samutpāda*), *śūnyatā* approaches the "non-original origin" that I have reinterpreted in terms of the divine milieu.[145]

What Taylor has missed is that co-dependent origination, or (co)dependent arising, is read in at least two ways in Buddhism. The conflict between presence (Altizer) and difference (Taylor) in postmodern theology seems to be mirrored in the debate between affirmative and negative readings of Nāgārjuna's (co)dependent arising in Buddhist studies. Since this latter negative reading requires difference and deferral rather than mutual co-dependence and relationality, it is probably more appropriate to omit the "co-" and talk of "dependent arising." It seems, then, that there is a "Buddhism of presence," co-dependent arising, and a "Buddhism of difference," dependent arising.

What follows is my understanding of the debate on (co)dependent arising and emptiness in Buddhist studies. Nāgārjuna felt the problem with the previous Buddhist position (in the Abhidharma texts) was twofold: it was possible to develop an attachment to dharmas as reified "things" and to emptiness as an absolute. He developed a two-part strategy to prevent this. In the first part he demonstrated that things are not independent but depend upon other things for their existence. For example, Nāgārjuna states:

> A thing is different insofar as it presupposes a second different thing.
> One thing is not different from another thing without the other thing.
> MMK 14.5[146]

In the second part of Nāgārjuna's strategy, he stressed that this dependence in fact empties things of inherent existence. This is Nāgārjuna's classic equation of interdependence, or "(co)dependent arising" and emptiness. He states:

> I have declared that which dependently co-arises to be emptiness. This
> is a descriptive designation having recourse [to dependent co-arising],
> and is the middle path. MMK 24:18[147]

The dominant scholarly reading of this verse is as follows: because things arise (co)dependently, they are empty (i.e. the reasoning here goes "(co)dependent arising therefore emptiness"). This reading of emptiness as (co)dependent arising seems to be the most popular scholarly reading of emptiness in Mahāyana Buddhism.

Finally, Nāgārjuna's strategies of "(co)dependent arising" and "emptying" must also be applied to emptiness itself. Nāgārjuna writes:

> If there were to be something non-empty, there would then be something
> called empty. However, there is nothing that is non-empty. How could
> there be something empty? MMK 13:7

> The Victorious Ones have announced that emptiness is the relinquishing
> of all views. Those who are possessed of the view of emptiness are said
> to be incorrigible. MMK 13:8[148]

"Emptiness," then, is (co)dependently arisen in the same way as everything else.

Yet while it is clear that things have no validity in themselves, can one say that they have a "dependent validity?"[149] One of Nāgārjuna's verses illustrates (co)dependent arising using the example of a father and a son. Nāgārjuna writes:

> If a son is produced by a father, and if that [father] is produced by that
> very son [when he is born],
> Then tell me, in this case, who produces whom? VV49[150]

It is by having a son that a father is produced. Therefore who is father to whom? In one sense it is the son who generates the father, or, to put it another way, a father arises only in (co)dependence with his son. Such a strategy "empties" concepts and categories of any independent existence.

But here is the question that marks the dispute: While "things" have no independent existence, do they exist in some mutual or reciprocal sense? Do father and son mutually create one another, or is the identity or presence of "father and son" always deferred because they are also linked to wife, mother, daughter, sister, brother, etc. In this latter case the work of emptiness is not the action of mutual affirmation but the action of endless deferral. Again, the conflict is between emptiness as a mutually established "position" or "presence" where things are always both negated and affirmed and emptiness as the absence or deferred presence of all positions. While the former reading seems compatible with Heidegger and presencing, the latter is closer to Taylor, Derrida and *différance*. One's position within this dispute has major consequences for understanding Buddhist practice and any notion of a "ground" for ethics.

Some scholars see the latter position (emptiness as difference, deferral and dependent arising) in the *prasanga* strain of Mādhyamika Buddhist thought. In his article "Is *Prasanga* a Form of Deconstruction?" Bimal Matilal explains:

> A *prasanga* argument is such that it is employed only to refute or reject
> a position; it does not involve the acceptance of the counter position or
> negation of a negative thesis. Those who employ only *prasanga* would
> not be prepared to concede any assertible thesis, positive or negative. In
> fact they would fault the negative or the counter thesis almost in the
> same way and almost as much as they fault the positive thesis.[151]

The logic here is not the dialectical "is not/is" of the first affirmative reading of co-dependent arising but rather something closer to "is not, is not, is not." The "truth" is that there is no truth..[152] Matilal suggests that there is a schism between those who pursue Buddhist practice as a means to "commitment" and those who pursue practice as a means to "denial."[153] Further, this difference is not limited to philosophical argumentation, but extends to "mental culture, or meditational praxis for meditating upon the Madhyamika truth, emptiness."[154] Clearly there is more than one reading of Buddhism here, each with its own understanding of the working of emptiness. While the working of presence may help explain the functioning of the first, it does not account for the second.

Although Taylor's work contains only a few references to Buddhism, similarities between his work and Buddhism have been pointed out by his reviewers, including Edith Wyschogrod, Toshihiko Izutsu and Thomas J.J. Altizer.[155] Many of these similarities are based on a view that Taylor's use of Derrida's *différance* (of difference and deferral) is similar to Nāgārjuna's two-part position on emptiness. The first part, that dependent arising can be equated with emptiness, can be read as the difference of *différance*, while the second part, that this emptiness is empty as well, can be read by philosophers of difference to be the deferral of *différance*.[156] While this reading of Nāgārjuna's emptiness may be compatible with the negative reading of sunyata as dependent arising, it is clearly incompatible with the positive reading of sunyata as co-dependent arising. Hence Taylor's critical article on Nishitani's affirmative presentation of co-dependence and emptiness.

From Taylor's perspective, the relationship between *sūnyatā* and *différance* is that both "can be understood as the differential that forms and deforms all differences. These differences, paradoxically, both constitute and subvert every identity."[157] "Deforms" and "subvert[s]" are the key terms here: the differential process of *différance* cannot be seen as a mutual establishment of identity.[158] While Taylor disagrees with Nishitani (and what I have called the Buddhism of presence, or presencing), he may be more approving of Matilal's reading of the use of prasanga in Buddhism (and what might be called a "Buddhism of difference"). Further, the growing movement of "Critical Buddhism" in Japan is also based on a "negative" reading of (co)dependent arising (as difference and deferral) and resonates somewhat with Taylor's work.[159]

3.4 The Sense of Difference (or the Grain of Nothing)

Is there a "sense" to nothing? One place to begin searching for such a "sense" is Taylor's "nO nOt nO," an article on negative theology. Taylor states:

> The return of, or to, negative theology is, in most cases, a gesture of recuperation. . . .All too often, the return to, or of, negative theology involves a dialectical move that is intended to negate negation. . . . It is precisely such gestures of recuperation that lead Derrida to deny that deconstruction is, in effect, a latter-day form of negative theology.[160]

Immediately after this critique of the "return to presence" in negative theology, Taylor continues with a comment on Derrida's "strange logic of No . . . not" ("No, what I write is not negative theology").[161] The double negative leaves open the possibility of an alternative reading. As Taylor puts it: "Disavowal is in some sense avowal. . . . The repressed always returns."[162]

But what about the ellipsis Taylor places between "No" and "not": " . . . "? Are these the "avowal" within "disavowal?" Do these mark the opening for the "return of the repressed?" They are reminiscent of Heidegger's use of the three dots in "Being in the presence of . . . ",[163] yet seem used in a different way. Are these three dots in "No . . . not" Derrida's or Heidegger's? And what of Taylor's use of them?

Taylor's use of the three dots demonstrates a different "working of nothing" from that of Heidegger. Taylor returns again and again to the three dots but it is at the end of the article (in his "p.s.") that they are most revealing. Instead of writing them horizontally as Heidegger does " . . . " Taylor turns them on their side

.

.

.

and "opens" them to make the mark of the empty space . . .

o

o

o

He repeats this series of three not just once, but three times. The gaps go on unendingly, the mark/hole/gap/difference/nothing is always deferred . . . . This shift in the marking of nothing (from Heidegger to Taylor) parallels the shift in the working of nothing from presence (or presencing) to difference (or differing). This is a new way of thinking nothing as the difference that always slides away.

What exactly is contained/repressed/returned in Taylor's unending three vertical dots/holes? Is there a sense or direction in Taylor's nothing? Is that part of its work? If nothing is not sense or direction in itself, perhaps it is the origin of sense and direction (not a cause, but perhaps a "cause"). *Dans le sens* means "with the grain." The notion of "grain" brings to mind Heidegger's woodworker. The skilled woodworker works with the grain (*dans le sens*) to allow the wood to be all it might be in its own being. The nature of the gift of the woodworker is then somewhat dependent on the nature of the grain of wood. Can Heidegger and Taylor be seen as workers of nothing? And if so, what is the "grain" of nothing, and how is it this "grain" differs from one to the other?

In the chapter on Lacan in *Altarity,* Taylor explores the "sense" of nothing through Lacan's use of "clinamen," a leaning, inclination or tendency. Is there a clinamen in Taylor's nothing? Taylor quotes from Lacan:

> "[The creation of the world] required a *clinamen*, an inclination, at some point. When Democritus tried to designate it . . . He said . . . *Nothing perhaps*? - not *perhaps nothing*, but *not nothing* [*Rien, peut-être*? *non pas - peut-être rien, mais pas rien*] (FFC 63-64; 61)."[164]

> [Taylor continues] The thing, perhaps, is no-thing, which "is" the nothing that seems to be the "cause" of all things.

> But what is a cause? There is no easy answer to this question, for, as Lacan stresses, a cause is a "hole" (*trou*), "cleft" (*fente*), or "gap" (*gap*) (*FFC*, 22;25) which has "the character of an absolute point without any knowledge" (*FFC*, 253; 228). "Whenever we speak of a cause . . . there is always something anti-conceptual, something indefinite. The phases of the moon are the cause of tides -- we know this from experience, we know the word cause is used correctly here. Or again, miasmas are the cause of fever -- that doesn't mean anything either, there is a hole, and something that oscillates in the interval. In short, there is a cause only in something *qui cloche*" (*FFC*, 22;25).[165]

There is an oscillation in the interval and a "something" in the oscillation. An "absolute point without any knowledge" but with, perhaps, a "cause."

Taylor's chapter on Blanchot (in *Altarity*) leads to an even stronger sense of leaning or "cause" in the gap/interval/nothing. Blanchot uses "*il*" ("it," neither masculine nor feminine) to refer to the neuter/difference/other. "It" is that which "'falls' (*tombe*) between all binary opposites."[166] Taylor quotes from Blanchot as follows:

> "Would it suffice nonetheless the say that (*il*), without having value or sense in itself, would permit all that inscribes itself in it to value or sense in itself, would permit all that inscribes itself in it to affirm itself in a determination that is always different?" (*PA*, 52)
> . . . In Blanchot's terms: ". . . Difference bears in its prefix the detour where all ability to give sense or direction searches for its origin in the gap that separates it" (*EI* 254).[167]

Again, the difference/neuter seems to act or function with a certain force to it. It gives birth to a sense, a direction. The "neuter" is then not completely "neutral."

Taylor continues with Blanchot's use of the myth of Orpheus and Eurydice. The "*il*" now becomes the "Orphic space."[168] The weight/bias/leaning in Orpheus's "nothing" is the absence of Eurydice. Even when Orpheus is not looking at her, "... in reality Orpheus has not ceased to be turned toward Eurydice."[169] This "turn" is the "force" in the nothing. It pulls or directs. It is the origin of the sense (or perhaps oscillation) which, in the end, turns Orpheus towards Eurydice. Perhaps this force is that which is repressed in Heidegger's three dots ("... ") and which returns in Taylor's holes (the vertical "o o o"). It seems, then, that the grain of nothing may well have an effect upon behaviour. But one wonders, is this grain a given? Can (or should) the grain of nothing be "altared"?

3.5 Difference and Ethics

> The origin of the work of art, in whose cleft Heidegger's Greek temple stands (and falls), is a certain *Riss* -- tear, tear, fissure, gap, flaw, crack. Perhaps this *Riss*, which rends the text of negative theology, points toward a different space and a different time. ... Perhaps the time/place of the *templum* is the time/place of a threshold that cannot be crossed or erased. Something like an invisible sieve, a filter that permits the eye to see.[170]

> The translator, in other words, does not exist in and for himself but is always for an other. He is a site of passage, something like a "sieve (*crible*)" that is forever straining .... Never speaking in his own voice, the translator echoes the discourse of an other.[171]

Perhaps Heidegger and Taylor are both translators. They are different "sites of passage," different "thresholds," or "filters," or "sieves" which strain that which they translate. Perhaps Heidegger and Taylor translate (filter/strain) nothing differently.

In "nO nOt nO" Taylor connects translation to thresholds. He writes:

> Remember, "we are still on the threshold." Not just here and now but always. The threshold is the site (or non-site/nonsight) of passage. But does a threshold permit translation (*trans*, across + *latus*, carried)? Can a passage, any passage, be translated?[172]

Here again we have "sites of passage" or "thresholds." Thresholds are "betweens" with two sides; a passage between some things and others. Some things cross (are translated) and others do not.

The question of ethics is this: if the self is a translator, a threshold or passage, what is the nature of the traffic it permits? What traffic does it obstruct? To make the stakes clear one must reveal what some of this traffic is. There are Nazis and (to use a non-Western example), the Japanese war machine on one or both sides of the threshold. Both groups are pressing to be carried across. If the Nazis are only on one side, then the direction of passage (the "grain" of the threshold) is crucial. If Nazis are on both sides, then it is not the direction but the shape/structure/nature (oscillation) in the passage that is vital. The nature of the passage allows some "things" to cross and not others. The nature of the passage allows some "things" to originate (through crossing) and not others. The stakes are high. To what does Taylor's passage give birth, and what does it abort?

Thresholds are all entry and exit points but differ from one another by what they close and/or connect. Is the question of ethics then the question of which way to move out of the threshold? I think not. As Taylor puts it: "Remember, 'we are still on the threshold.' Not just here and now but always."[173] If one is always on the threshold then perhaps the question of ethics is better put as questioning the nature of one's own threshold. For thresholds are, of course, "nothings of transition" which structure (sieve or "strain") that which passes through. The question regarding the nature of the three dots/holes is now an ethical question: How does the grain of the threshold orient one's world? What does it allow through?

This sense of "threshold" and "nothing" is similar to Heidegger's "jug," whose gift is in its pouring forth. "'The jug's jug-character consists in the poured gift of the pouring out.' (*PLT* 172) The jug gives. . . *Es gibt*. . . a gift. . . *un don*."[174] One can know something of the nature of a threshold by that which it pours forth or translates.

But the question is not so much "what does it mean to translate Heidegger?"[175] as "what does it mean to translate nothing?" For, if one is not careful, if one does not take care in the translation, then Nazis may slip through the door.

But how to take care? Perhaps through questioning the nature of the "filter" or "sieve," for in doing so one questions the nature of one's engagement of the world.[176] If the "filter" is the means by which we engage the world, "a filter that permits the eye to see,"[177] is it possible to change the filter? Again, can the grain of nothing be altered?

First, however, one must be aware of what it is that passes through the filter/sieve or across the passage/threshold. Again, one returns to the nature of the sense or leaning in Taylor's nothing. Perhaps, in order to reflect this leaning, Taylor's neuter or median in the and/or which joins/divides should be written not as a line or a slash, but as a curve: there is a curve or swerve to difference. And/or and self/

other is then always read with a leaning, and it is the nature of this leaning that distinguishes Taylor from Heidegger (and may indicate a basis for a difference in "filters" and subsequent behaviour). The slash " / " may be better written as ") ", leaning one way or the other to indicate weight or bias: in the and/or Heidegger leans toward the "and" -- and ") " or -- whereas Taylor leans toward the "or" -- and " (" or.

One of Taylor's quotations from Heidegger can be used to illustrate this point. Taylor quotes:

> The strife is not a tear [*Riss*] as the gaping crack [*Ausfreissen*] of a pure cleft [*Kluft*], but the strife is the intimacy [*Innigkeit*] with which combatants belong to each other. This tear pulls the opponents together in the origin [*Herkunft*] of their unity by virtue of their common ground.[178]

I read Taylor on one side of the "tear" and Heidegger on the other: Taylor is strife ") " intimacy while Heidegger is opponents " (" unity.

It is this leaning towards the "or" of and/or that may provide the basis for a discussion of the question of ethics with regard to Taylor's thought. One way in which the subject of ethics can be approached is as an investigation of the relation of self to other, or as an analysis of the thinking framework that accounts for sameness/difference in the relation of self/ other. The line "between" self/other ("/") is, of course, the gap/interval/abyss/opening/nothing. But the work of this nothing differs in Heidegger and Taylor. The line between seems to be used to gather for Heidegger, and (almost) to separate in Taylor.

There may be even one more way of viewing this difference. The line that separates and joins self/other may also be represented with Heidegger's use of horizontal dots (to indicate presence) and Taylor's use of vertical dots (to indicate difference and deferral). This would involve two different re-drawings of the cleaving sign.

For Heidegger: "self . . . other."

For Taylor: "self

                o

                o

                o

                        other."

This can be stretched even a little further for the Taylor of the Levinas chapter in *Altarity*. In addressing the difference between Gadamer and Derrida, John Caputo suggests contrasting images of a tennis game might be useful.[179] For Gadamer, the game might be played on clay or grass but the object would be to keep the ball in play. For Derrida/Levinas, however, the game might be seen played on a court where the two sides are at uneven levels: the side of the other is at a level higher than the side of the self. The self would then always in a position of serving up.

I do not think it too much of a reach to bring Taylor into this game as well. His three dots, or "drawing" holes, could also be seen as a tennis ball being played back and forth. If so, then the above example of the relation between self and other could be re-drawn once more. Perhaps:

> other
>
> o
>
>   o
>
>   o
>
>   self.

Nothing here has weight and force. Further, there is a bias, a swerve. (There may be a spin on the ball, a little enthusiasm.) One must always be ready to respond. Perhaps, then, the work of difference contains within it, as part of its being, a claim or a demand on the relation between self and other: one's response must always be in keeping with the s(w)erve of the other.

This s(w)erve of the other puts the interaction between self and other in a different light. As Taylor has put it:

> In the play of paralectics, the dialectical struggle for mastery gives way
> to the patient suffering of the unmasterable dis-course of the other.[180]

Taylor's earlier work in *Erring* (1984) contains a number of passages that point towards a possible position on ethical action. Taylor writes:

> For the needy self, lack is not primal; rather it is secondary to more
> original plenitude. Lack, therefore, represents a *deficiency* that one must
> strive to overcome. The subject in need always seeks fulfillment or
> satisfaction. The achievement of satisfaction, it is believed, will put an
> end to deficiency by *restoring* plenitude.
>
> Need, however, is misguided. . . . The subject that has discovered its
> own impropriety realizes that the wound that the needy self takes to be
> secondary is actually primal. Instead of a negated presence, absence is
> interior to presence and is "in" the present "from the beginning."[181]

This is akin to the earlier discussion on the possibility of "total presence" for which the Fontana painting was used as an illustration. Seeing the lack as an integral part of our being may completely change our understanding of ourselves. Taylor writes:

> In contrast to the needy self, which yearns for completion, the desiring subject does not want fulfillment. The subject that desires is never satiated and yet is neither dissatisfied nor unhappy. *Desire desires desire*. Having realized that death is in life and life in death, that presence is in absence and absence in presence, the empty subject no longer seeks the satisfaction that fills, completes, and closes.[182]

Further, when the self is understood in this different way, it becomes possible to approach life, and the others in one's life, in a new way. Taylor continues:

> . . . if the lack is "original" and not secondary, then it is not necessarily a deficiency. Furthermore, if lack entails no deficiency, one might become free of the dreadful need to overcome it. If the subject does not need to repress the other "within," it is not driven to oppress the other "without."[183]

The last line seems to be the key: an acceptance of "difference" within may well lead to an acceptance of "difference" without. From the perspective of difference any ethic of presence is an attempt to close or fuse this gap/difference and to negate otherness. Recognizing the primacy of the lack leads to bowing to the s(w)erve of the other.

However, this is as close as Taylor comes to suggesting that the internal work of difference might, or should, have an effect on one's external actions. For to move further requires turning difference into Difference -- process has turned into product and is no longer *différance*. When this is done, the "ethics of Difference" seems to suffer from the same flaw as the "ethics of presence": there seems to be no necessary connection between acceptance of the internal position and external action. The connection between *différance* and a "regard for Otherness" seems to me theological rather than logical, a matter of faith or preference rather than of logical necessity. This is not to negate the importance or value of any ethics of Difference (I think it is important and should be developed further), but to question the claim that it is somehow grounded in a manner more legitimate than any ethics of presence. Accepting the work of difference in the process of thinking does not compel one to respect difference in relating to others. Or, to reverse the point, the internal working of difference is not dependent on any particular external action.

A Buddhism of difference not only faces this important question of ethical ground but one other as well: what happens to enlightenment here? How does one account for Dōgen's "whole being is Buddha nature," or "dropping off body and mind"?

4 THE WORKING OF ESSENCE: TATHĀGATAGARBHA THOUGHT, DŌGEN KIGEN AND BUDDHA NATURE

The Essence (of the Buddha) is (by nature) devoid (śūnya)
Of the accidental (pollutions) which differ from it;
But it is by no means devoid (aśūnya) of the highest properties
Which are, essentially, indivisible from it.
        -- the Ratnagotravibhāga[184]

. . . is not the Ratnagotra's fourfold attribution of the Dharmakaya as supreme
bliss, supreme eternity, supreme unity, and supreme purity totally opposed by
the Mādhyamikan śūnyatā-śūnyatā, an absolute insistence on the indeterminate
nature of the unconditioned reality?
        -- Brian Edward Brown[185]

Whole being is the Buddha-nature.
        -- Dōgen[186]

In the preceding chapters Buddhist emptiness has been presented as opposed
views of (co)dependent arising. The first reading of emptiness (in the Buddhism
section of the chapter on Heidegger and presencing) sees co-dependent arising as
an "emptying" and affirming process (the positive dialectical logic of "is not/is").
The second reading of emptiness (in the Buddhism section of the chapter on Mark
Taylor and difference) sees dependent arising as a process of endless negation and
deferral (a negative dialectical logic closer to "is not/is not"). Both of these positions
can cite Nāgārjuna as an authority for their reading of emptiness.

Yet something has been overlooked in these two readings: the logic of
negation --whether positive (co-dependent arising) or negative (dependent arising)
-- does not adequately explain the Buddha nature or Buddha essence literature in
the Buddhist tradition. Indeed, some Buddhist texts have a conception of emptiness
that seems clearly opposed to the (co)dependent arising readings of scholars who
rely on Nāgārjuna and the Mādhyamika school. This is most apparent in the

Tathāgatagarbha literature and has been noted by scholars of both the co-dependent arising and dependent arising positions. From the perspective of the latter position, Robert Gimello asks:

> Among modern European, American, Indian, and Japanese scholars, it has long been the common assumption, if not always the explicitly advanced thesis, that Mahāyāna Buddhist thought reached a kind of philosophical pinnacle in the expostulation of Mādhyamika. . . . Now if Prasangika Mādhyamika were truly the summit of Mahāyāna thought, and if that summit were, as has been alleged, no philosophical view in itself but only a rigorously negative dialectic by which all false views -- meaning, all views -- are deconstructed and shown to be null, then one might wonder . . . what is to be done, for example, with the characteristic Mahāyāna assertion that all sentient beings possess the Buddha nature? How can this be so, or what can this mean, if all sentient beings are also empty. . . ?[187]

Perhaps, then, one can acknowledge the importance of dependent arising in Buddhism while denying that it need be ultimate or absolute in Buddhist thought and practice.[188] One wonders, must śūnyatā be read as a variant of (co)dependent arising in all places and at all times?

A scholar of the positive co-dependent arising position, Gadjin Nagao, states flatly that the use and function of emptiness in the Tathāgatagarbha literature cannot be embraced within his understanding of the term. In commenting on the *Ratnagotra* (one of the key Tathāgatagarbha texts), he writes:

> In the *Ratnagotra* . . . one subtracts defilements from the Tathāgatagarbha and the remaining difference is Buddhahood. . . . In such subtraction, one cannot see the dialectical double character that is fundamentally the character of emptiness, and whose basic meaning is expressed in the concept of emptiness. . . .Thus, one cannot but have doubts concerning the *Ratnagotra's* usage of [emptiness].[189]

Although the last sentence indicates that Nagao is clearly among those who read Buddhism through co-dependent arising, this does not negate his main point: there is quite another view of emptiness in the Buddhist tradition and this emptiness works in a way completely different from the emptiness of co-dependent arising. While I agree with Nagao that the "logic of śūnyatā" in the *Ratnagotra* is different, I disagree (as will become clear below) with his presupposition that there is only one correct or legitimate understanding of the work of emptiness in the entire Buddhist tradition.

Nagao introduces the term "subtraction" here to distinguish the working of emptiness in Tathāgatagarbha thought from the dialectical working of emptiness associated with co-dependent arising and Mādhyamika -- defilements are not presenced but subtracted and it is through the practice of subtraction that one reaches Buddhahood. This chapter draws on Nagao's use of subtraction but uses the term "essence" or "Buddha essence" to describe that which is revealed through subtraction. The third working of emptiness is then a two-step process of subtraction/essence (or rather one process with two aspects). "Tathāgatagarbha" can be translated as the germ, seed, embryo or essence (*garbha*) of the "thus gone one" or Buddha (Tathāgata).[190] I use "Buddha essence" as a rendering of "Tathāgatagarbha," because this usage also lends itself well to a re-reading of Dōgen's work.

There are two main points made in the Tathāgatagarbha texts that seem to suggest a subtraction/essence reading of emptiness.[191] First, there are two wisdoms of *śūnyatā*: the wisdom of the emptiness of defilements and impurities and the wisdom of the non-emptiness or positive nature of the essence of the Tathāgata. While *śūnyatā* is empty with regard to defilements, it is non-empty with regard to virtues.

Second, rather than the logic of negation of the (co)dependent arising readings of emptiness, there is a logic of subtraction where defilements are subtracted (because they are empty) leaving only virtues (which are non-empty). This differing logic is what distinguishes the Buddha essence reading of emptiness from the affirmative reading of co-dependent arising. While in the co-dependent arising reading (associated with presencing) the same subject both "is" and "is not," in Tathāgatagarbha thought the subject of negation (is not) and affirmation (is) is completely different. While defilements are subtracted, they are not affirmed. While the virtues of the second wisdom of emptiness are affirmed, they are never negated.

This is a crucial point. Any notion of subtraction in meditation practice is incompatible with the position in co-dependent arising and presencing that everything simultaneously "is" and "is not": if a thing is to be subtracted, then it cannot be true that it both "is not" and "is," only that it "is not."[192] (As will become clear later on, this becomes especially critical when discussing how one deals with karma in meditation practice.) In the Buddhist language of the two truths, it is quite possible to accept dependent arising as the conventional truth while seeing Buddha essence as the absolute truth. From this perspective -- what I am calling the third reading of the working of emptiness -- the realization of emptiness is not the realization of things which are empty but the realization of emptiness alone.[193] Forms, whether emptied or not, are not primary in this third understanding of emptiness.

Regarding the "genuine" meaning of *śūnyatā*, then, there seem to be three possibilities: affirmative co-dependent arising (working as presencing); negative dependent arising (working as differing and deferring); and Buddha essence (which does not refute dependent arising, but does not see it as primary).

Clearly, these different positions on emptiness will lead to quite different readings of Dōgen.[194] In my view, both (co)dependent arising readings suffer from serious drawbacks. The positive co-dependent arising reading, while highlighting Dōgen's dialectical strategies, does not adequately account for either the relationship between meditation and karma in Dōgen or the two-step approach to practice Dōgen seems to advocate in his writings.[195] The negative dependent arising reading (e.g. in the Critical Buddhism movement) cannot embrace Buddha nature or enlightenment. (These points will be clarified later in the chapter.) The Buddha essence reading of Dōgen offers a third possibility, and is that which will be explored in this chapter.

I have found the Tathāgatagarbha concept of the two wisdoms of emptiness very helpful in developing this Buddha essence reading of Dōgen. My suggestion is that accounting for the difference between the "two wisdoms of emptiness" (i.e. the wisdom of the empty and the wisdom of the non-empty) may be one way of reading Dōgen's "two aspects of studying the way" (explained below) and of distinguishing between the zazen of the student and the zazen of the Master. In both cases, the first aspect or first wisdom is seen as incomplete or partial and in need of the second to be true. I will argue that such a reading has the advantage of being able to address the place of karma and enlightenment in Dōgen.

The claim in this chapter is threefold: first, that there is a subtraction/essence reading of emptiness in the Buddhism of the Tathāgatagarbha literature; second, that Dōgen can be read through subtraction/essence more legitimately than through (co)dependent arising (whether positive or negative);[196] and third, that a successful attempt to read Dōgen through Buddha essence has larger implications -- that it can inspire and "ground" a Buddhist philosophy of essence (to be outlined in the next chapter). This chapter, then, is an attempt to provide a textual base within Buddhism to support the more constructive workings of the next chapter.

4.1 Subtraction and Essence in Tathāgatagarbha Thought

Among the scriptures understood to represent the Tathāgatagarbha tradition are the *Śrimālā sūtra* (third century C.E.), the *Lankāvatāra sūtra* (fourth century C.E.), the *Ratnagotravibhāga sūtra*, and the Awakening of Faith. The two wisdoms of emptiness are prominently mentioned in the *Śrimālā sūtra*, which is cited in the

Lankāvatāra and *Ratnagotravibhāga sūtras* (and may well be a source for the *Awakening of Faith*).[197] The key passage of the scripture reads as follows:

> O Lord, there are two kinds of wisdom of Emptiness with reference to the Tathagatagarbha.
> O Lord, 1) the Tathāgatagarbha which is Empty is separate from, free from, and different from the stores of all defilements.
> O Lord, 2) the Tathāgatagarbha which is not empty is not separate from, not free from, and not different from the inconceivable Buddhadharmas, more numerous than the sands of the Ganges.
> O Lord, the various great Śrāvakas can believe in the Tathāgata with reference to the two wisdoms of Emptiness.[198]

The Tathāgatagarbha is then empty with respect to defilements but not empty with respect to the virtues of Buddhahood. Further, the knowledge of the empty and the knowledge of the non-empty are each referred to as one of the "wisdoms of Emptiness."

The *Ratnagotravibhāga sūtra* has very strong links to the *Śrimālā sūtra*, citing it more than any other: all the citations come from approximately a third of the sutra, the section including and surrounding the passages discussing emptiness.[199] The *Ratnagotra's* central passage on emptiness reads as follows:

> The Essence (of the Buddha) is (by nature) devoid (*śūnya*)
> Of the accidental (pollutions) which differ from it;
> But it is by no means devoid (*aśūnya*) of the highest properties
> Which are, essentially, indivisible from it.[200]

It would seem, then, that there are two aspects of emptiness, each of which needs to be understood. Following the *Śrimālā sūtra*, I will continue to refer to these as the "two wisdoms of emptiness."

One of the *Ratnagotra's* goals is to present these two wisdoms of emptiness as an explicit critique of earlier understandings of emptiness (which present only one wisdom). The *Ratnagotra* counters this "mistake" by demonstrating the positive qualities of *śunyātā*, the second wisdom of emptiness. This critique is expressed most clearly in chapter eleven of the *Ratnagotra*, "The Purpose of Instruction." It asks, if everything is "'unreal', like clouds, (visions in) a dream," then "why has the Buddha declared here/ That the Essence of the Buddhas 'exists' in every living being?"[201] Interestingly enough, this is very close to the question of Robert Gimello (mentioned earlier): If all views are null and void, what does one do with the view that all beings have the Buddha Nature? The scripture continues a little later in the same chapter:

If a man of intelligence perceives (only)
That the defects (of living beings) are unreal,
And depreciates (their) virtues which are real,
He cannot obtain benevolence by which
One regards (other) living beings as equal to oneself.[202]

The problem seems to be one of incorrect focus. By attending only to the emptiness of the defects (the first wisdom), the student does not see the true Buddha essence (the second wisdom). Again, while the defects or defilements may be unreal or empty, the virtues are not.

Chapter nine of the *Ratnagotra,* "The 9 illustrations of the germ covered with defilements," explains the relationship between defilements and Buddha essence. It reads (in part):

Like the Buddha in an ugly lotus flower
Like honey surrounded by bees,
Like kernels of grains covered by the husk,
Like gold fallen into impurities,
Like a treasure under the ground,
Like a sprout, . . . grown from a small fruit,
Like an image of the Buddha wrapped in a tattered garment,

Like the kinghood in the womb of a poor woman,
And like a precious statue in the earthen mould;
In such a way, there abides this Essence
In the living beings obscured by occasional stains of defilements.[203]

The sūtra goes on to discuss each of the illustrations individually. The bees/honey illustration, for example, is further clarified: "The Defilements are like honey-bees, and the Essence of the Tathāgata is akin to the honey." One needs to establish the difference between the two and then "drive the bees away" before making use of the honey.[204]

With reference to the two wisdoms of emptiness, the first wisdom would be knowledge of the "emptiness" of bees, impurities and ground (earth); the second wisdom would be an understanding of the positive nature of honey, gold and treasure. Defilements are seen as pollutions which hide the true nature of the essence of the Tathāgata. A problem arises when the student focuses so exclusively on the emptiness of defects that access to knowledge of virtues is blocked: defects end up being indirectly affirmed (through attention) rather than subtracted. The student should shift focus and attempt to dwell on, or in, virtues.[205] Buddha essence is then not the emptiness of the bees, but the positive nature of honey.

In an example similar to the one of "bees and honey," practice is likened to digging for gold:

> Just as gold is not seen when covered by pebbles and sand and is seen by due purification, likewise the Tathāgata in the world.[206]

It is important to note here that the pebbles are not dialectically negated, whether presenced, or "emptied" through the logic of "is/is not" -- they are washed away. It is only after this subtraction that the "gold," the unconditioned bliss or purity of the second wisdom of emptiness, can be found.

To sum up, the Tathāgatagarbha is not seen by ordinary people as it is hidden from view by defilements. These defilements are not dialectically negated ("is/is not") but dissolve (or are subtracted) in meditation practice. At this point Buddha essence is revealed. There are then two steps involved which correspond to the two wisdoms of emptiness: first, defilements are subtracted (because they are empty); second, attention or awareness is shifted from defilements to essence. This essence is the genuine śūnyatā.

4.2 Subtraction and Essence in Dōgen

Within Dōgen's writings, the work of emptiness as subtraction seems most apparent in his discussion of meditation and the "five desires" or the "five defilements" in the Hōkyōki (Dōgen's journal from his years in China).[207] Dōgen relates the words of his teacher as follows:

> When practicing singleminded intense sitting, the five desires will depart and the five defilements will be removed.[208]

And a little later:

> Unless you eliminate the three poisons and the five desires, you are identical to the heretics in the country of Bimbisara and Ajatasatru. If the descendants of the buddhas and patriarchs eliminate even a single defilement or desire, they will benefit greatly; this is the moment of direct encounter with the buddhas and patriarchs.[209]

Here the work of meditation seems to involve the elimination (or subtraction) of the five desires (the desire for wealth, sex, food and drink, fame, and sleep) and the five defilements (craving, anger, sleep, regret, and doubt).[210]

Later Dōgen returns to the subject when he ascribes the following words to his teacher:

> The descendants of the buddhas and patriarchs eliminate first the five defilements and then the sixth. Adding the defilement of nescience to the five defilements constitutes the six defilements. By simply eliminating nescience, you have eliminated [all] five defilements. If you have departed from the five defilements but not nescience, you have not yet reached the cultivation and experience of the buddhas and patriarchs.[211]

As Kodera mentions in a footnote, for Dōgen's teacher the purpose of zazen is not "the attainment of buddhahood, but . . . the removal of the five desires and defilements."[212]

It is worth noting here that in the Waddell translation of the *Hōkyōki*, the second term is not "defilements," but "restraints" or "covers" (*gogai*),[213] which suggests a comparison to the *Ratnagotra's* example of pebbles and sand covering gold (defilements covering Buddha essence). From the subtraction/essence perspective, emptiness is then not a property of the "covers" at all (i.e. that they are co-dependently arisen), but an essence that is discovered when the covers are removed or subtracted. Again, this is different from the position that meditation is a simultaneous negation and affirmation, "is not/is," or presencing of whatever is at hand.

Another reference which seems to support the work of subtraction in Dōgen is the fascicle "Shizenbiku" ("A Monk at the Fourth Stage of Meditation"). Here Dōgen discusses the different stages of becoming an arahat, and the thoughts and behaviour that mark each stage. Dōgen tells two stories in which monks realize that they had overestimated their attainments in Buddhist practice. They come to these realizations by observing that their immediate instinctual response to external conditions is not that of a fourth stage arahat.

In the first example, Dōgen relates a story about Upagupta and one of his disciples. He states:

> One of the Venerable Upagupta's disciples . . . mistakenly believed he had also realized Arahathood when he attained the fourth stage of meditation. In order to correct his mistaken belief, Upagupta told him to travel to a certain area. Upagupta then used his supernatural power to create an incident that his disciple would encounter along the way.
> The incident involved a group of five hundred merchants who were attacked and killed by a band of robbers. When the disciple saw their bodies strewn here and there, he was overcome with fear and suddenly

thought to himself, "I guess I have not realized Arhathood after all; I must still be at the third stage."[214]

In this example, it was enough that fear of his own mortality arose to indicate to the monk that he was not an Arahat.

Dōgen elaborates on this point in a second story later in "Shizenbiku." Here a monk is dominated first by anger and then by sexual desire. The monk . . .

> . . . thought he must at least have attained Arahathood. When someone subsequently criticized him, however, he became angry and thus realized that he had not achieved Arahathood either, though he was still convinced that at the very least he had achieved the third stage (to Arahathood). When he saw a young woman, however, he was filled with sexual desire, and finally realized he had not even achieved the first stage. It was due to his knowledge of the Buddha's teaching that he realized his shortcomings.[215]

Here again the actions of the monk were determined by the emotions that arose. There is a difference between noticing that anger is arising and becoming angry. In becoming angry the monk stepped out of the practice of meditation. In the case of a monk more mature in practice this would not be the case.

But there is a larger issue being addressed in these two stories. It would seem that at a certain stage of meditation practice anger, fear and lust are simply no longer a part of one's instinctual or intuitive response to the presence or absence of external conditions. Anger, fear and lust are dependent on false notions of self and existence, and once these false notions dissolve through meditation, it may be that anger, fear and lust no longer arise. The presence or absence of anger (one of the five defilements), for example, would then act as a way to check on the maturity of a monk's practice. The monks in these stories know this, and it is this knowledge that enables them (eventually) to achieve Arahathood.

It would seem, then, that it is not that the enlightened being has all the fears, anxieties and worries of the normal person, only less so, or is not attached to them, but rather that his or her entire affective mode has changed. Those who read co-dependent arising as primary may suggest that there is a non-attachment to fear or anger in emptiness, but they are logically precluded from suggesting that these are somehow transformed or eliminated for then fear or anger could not be both "is" and "is not." This is a vital point, and relates directly to the legitimacy of the two readings of emptiness. In the subtraction/essence working of emptiness, the behaviour of an enlightened being is less related to external events than to a transformed internal affective mode. Anger and fear are dependent on the presence or absence of external conditions -- these emotions are, themselves, external to essence. Focusing attention on defilements (restraints, covers, externals) blocks sensitivity to, and awareness of, what lies beneath defilements. Only when defilements have been subtracted can a completely different type of response arise from the thus revealed Buddha essence. In the Buddha essence reading of emptiness, presencing anger and fear blocks the path to enlightenment -- it is an extremely serious mistake in practice.

4.3 The Two Aspects of Zen Practice as Subtraction and Essence

Dōgen's discussion of the "two aspects of practice" in *Gakudō Yōjinshū* (*Guidelines for Studying the Way*) also suggests that emptiness works as subtraction/ essence.[216] The first aspect of practice, working toward "cutting the root of thinking," could be seen as the work of subtraction, while the second aspect, Dōgen's "dropping off of body and mind," could be a shift in what is primary -- from the "emptiness of the covers" to the awareness of Buddha essence. Dōgen introduces the two aspects by stating that a person studies the way . . .

> by sitting, which severs the root of thinking and blocks access to the road of intellectual understanding. This is an excellent means to arouse true beginner's mind. Then you let body and mind drop away and let go of delusion and enlightenment. This is the second aspect of studying the way.
> Generally speaking, those who trust that they are within the buddha way are most rare. If you have correct trust that you are within the buddha way, you understand where the great way leads or ends, and you know the original source of delusion and enlightenment. If once, in sitting, you sever the root of thinking, in eight or nine cases out of ten you will immediately attain understanding of the way.[217]

Dōgen is clear: studying the way has at least two aspects. The first aspect, zazen or sitting, may "sever the root of thinking," but this is not the whole of practice, it is just the beginning ("an excellent means to arouse true beginner's mind"). The second aspect is that "body and mind drop away." Although both of these aspects are a part of the long-term practice of zazen, the two aspects are not the same. This, to me, supports a two-step reading of Dōgen's Zen practice. In my reading it is the dissolution or subtraction of the five hindrances or five desires (karma) in the first step that prepares the way for the second step -- a sudden shift in what is primary in orienting perception from defilements to essence.

Support for such a two-step reading of Zen practice can also be found in the "Zazenshin" fascicle. The first part of the fascicle centers on the story of the monk polishing the tile. While this story had traditionally been used to illustrate the futility of trying to achieve Buddhahood by doing zazen (polishing the tile), Dōgen completely shifts the emphasis of the story by situating the conversation not before but <u>after</u> the sitting monk's realization (after the experience of "dropping off body and mind"). From this new perspective the monk's sitting in ceaseless zazen is not an attempt to realize the "truth," but the actual manifestation of enlightenment. This is one source of Dōgen's classic equation of practice and enlightenment.

This part of the fascicle, however, can only be understood in the context of what follows later, where Dōgen equates zazen with the transmission of the truth from Master to disciple. Dōgen again distinguishes between two aspects, or two types of zazen: zazen in general and zazen based upon the transmission of the Buddhas and patriarchs:

> Generally, the transmission of the Law always means that of *zabutsu* [becoming a Buddha], because *zabutsu* is the essential function (of zazen). Without the transmission of the Law, no zazen would have been transmitted. It is only this essence of zazen that has been transmitted from master to disciple. Without the personal transmission of this essence, there cannot be the Buddhas and patriarchs; without a clear grasp of this one (zazen) they will remain ignorant of all things and deeds. In this case they cannot be said to have clarified the Law or realized the Way, still less the Buddhas and patriarchs, ancient and modern. ... All monks from the chief monk to trainees regard zazen as their original duty, persuading others to do zazen. But nevertheless few chief monks are aware of (true) zazen.[218]

All monks may do zazen, but not all zazen is the transmission of the Law. The zazen of the beginner may not be the same as the zazen of the Zen Master. This statement of Dōgen suggests that the equation of practice and enlightenment might be linked accurately with only the second aspect of practice.

Many of Dōgen's lectures in the *Shōbōgenzō* can be read as an attempt to invoke a perspectival shift in his monks from the first aspect of practice to the second. Again, I read this as a shift in what is primary, from "cutting the root of thinking" to "dropping off body and mind." The very first fascicle of the *Shōbōgenzō*, the "Genjōkōan" ("Manifesting Absolute Reality") contains two well-known examples which seem to suggest such a shift:

Conveying the self to myriad things to authenticate them is delusion; the myriad things advancing to authenticate the self is enlightenment. . . . To be authenticated by the myriad things is to drop off the mind-body of oneself and others.[219]

When a man goes off in a boat and looks back at the shoreline, he mistakenly thinks the shore is moving. If he keeps his eyes closely on his boat, he realizes it is the boat that is advancing. In a like manner, when a person [tries to] discern and affirm the myriad dharmas with a confused conception of [his own] body and mind, he mistakenly thinks his own mind and his own nature are permanent. If he makes all his daily deeds intimately his own and returns within himself, the reason that the myriad dharmas are without self will become clear to him.[220]

Although this perspectival shift happens in an instant, the preparation for this shift may be long and arduous. Dōgen writes:

When you finally achieve the various liberations by doing zazen, everything that was held from you in the past because of your discriminating mind will be revealed to you at once. This instant of revelation of reality. . . [221]

I equate "finally achieve the various liberations by doing zazen" with the first aspect of practice and "instant revelation of reality" with the second. In "Dōtoku," Dōgen writes:

. . . one drops off those months and years of effort. When you drop them off, the dropping off of skin, flesh, bones and marrow is likewise experienced, and earth, mountains and rivers are experienced as dropped off. . . . at the time of this dropping off, expression is immediately manifested.[222]

Here I equate "those months and years of effort" with the first aspect of practice (cutting the root of thinking) and "at the time of this dropping off, expression is immediately manifested" with the second aspect (dropping off body and mind). Buddhist practice matures from subtraction of defilements to realization of essence.

4.4 A Poetic Digression: The Legend of the Sixth Patriarch

The two aspects of practice seem also to be the issue in the two poems surrounding the legend of the sixth Patriarch. The story that provides the context for the poems goes as follows: the Fifth Patriarch of Zen Buddhism in China was looking for a successor and asked his students to write a poem demonstrating their understanding. One poem was written on a wall in a public place; later a second one was added. These poems read:

Shen Hsiu: The body is the Bodhi tree,
               The mind is like a clear mirror.
               At all times we must strive to polish it,
               And must not let the dust collect.

Hui Neng: Bodhi originally has no tree,
               The mirror also has no stand.
               From the beginning not a thing is,
               Where is there room for dust?[223]

The first poem can be read as an expression of "cutting the root of thinking" (the first aspect of practice or the first wisdom of emptiness). The second poem can be read as an expression of "dropping off body and mind" (the second aspect of practice or the second wisdom of emptiness). In the story the Fifth Patriarch praises the first poem, as do all the students, but states clearly that it falls short of true understanding:

> This verse you wrote shows that you still have not reached true understanding. You have merely arrived at the front gate but have yet to be able to enter it. If common people practice according to your verse, they will not fail. But in seeking the ultimate enlightenment (bodhi) one will not succeed with such an understanding. You must enter the gate and see your own original nature.[224]

The Fifth Patriarch seems to be saying that while the first poem might be good instruction for a beginner ("if common people practice according to your verse they will not fail"), it is not the whole of practice. This is reminiscent of Dōgen's statement that "cutting the root of thinking" is an "excellent means to arouse true beginner's mind," but only the first aspect of practice. It is the author of the second poem who becomes the Sixth Patriarch.

I see the first poem as a more or less traditional working of "the self is empty" (a working consistent with a "Buddhism of presencing"). In its original state the self is empty like a clear mirror. Yet this clear state is often obscured by the debris of personal opinions and ideas. A cluttered, dusty mirror-self does not allow a pure experience of reality. Dropping strong opinions and ideas about things is necessary in order to experience the brilliant intensity of life-as-it-is. By practicing meditation diligently, the debris on the mirror is gradually cleaned away. Keeping up meditation practice keeps the mirror clean and allows a "presencing" of the world just as it is. The pure cry of a bird, the subtle and transient beauty of the cherry blossoms -- these things are now perceived directly, without the dust of personal opinions obscuring one's experience.

The clarity of this mirror reflects and is reflected in other mirrors. Therefore whatever appears in one's own mirror-self is contingent on the state of other mirror selves. Any one "self" is inextricably bound up with all other "selves." There can be no separate selves when each individual self is at least partly constructed in relationship with others.

From the perspective of the first poem (the self is empty), the problem is discrimination between and attachment to things that are ultimately empty. As meditation practice deepens the solution appears: it is not that things are "real" but that things are empty. One understands the illusory nature of things and is no longer attached to them (for how can one be attached to things that are empty?). Although one may continue to perceive (cut or "cise" and draw forth) in a similar way, one's understanding of these perceptions has completely changed: these perceptions are "empty."

But this is the first poem and "the self is empty," the "months and years of effort" involved in cutting the root of thinking. The difficulty of "the self is empty" is that it is easy to see the self as a frame that has not been filled in. Perceptions weave in and out, and come and go within the frame. But from the perspective of the second poem this is at best incomplete. This is not the "not believing in a self" but the belief in a "no-self." In other words, when seeing the self as empty one continues to select, inscribe or "draw" self first. Leaving the inscribed self blank is a secondary action dependent on the original inscription. The point is this: one's orientation is primarily determined by the original inscription rather than by whether or not one fills in the blank.

The move from the first poem to the second can be seen as a shift from "the self is empty" to "emptiness is the self." From the perspective of the second poem (emptiness is the self), the solution of the first poem (the self is empty) is still seen to be part of the problem; an enlightened perspective would require one more step. As the Fifth Patriarch pointed out, "If common people practice according to your verse, they will not fail. But in seeking the ultimate enlightenment (bodhi) one will not succeed with such an understanding."

Perhaps the idea is not to see the same things and then understand them differently but to see differently in the first place. From this second perspective the problem is not attachment to things, but creation of things. The problem is not discrimination between things but their very formation in the first place. It is not that a Buddhist with a mature practice thinks, sees and senses the same way as before but is not attached. Rather, it is that Buddhist practice changes thinking, seeing and sensing radically and that non-attachment follows as a by-product of this change. It is not that there are forms out there, and the Buddhist is not attached to them. It is that for the Buddhist forms are no longer primary.

As the second poem goes, "From the beginning not a thing is." It follows that if one sees differently, a different understanding will result. However, one arrives at this different understanding not by thinking differently about the relationships between what one sees, but by proceeding from a completely different starting point. If forms are not primary, then it is misleading even to speak of non-attachment within emptiness. It is only people observing the Buddhist action of the second poem from within the perceptual field of the first poem who would speak in these terms.   Discriminating less between me and not-me does not necessarily lead to the dissolution of "me" and "not-me." Becoming less and less attached to "others" does not need to result in the dissolution of "others" as a perceptual construct.

This is not to say that the first poem does not enrich and deepen one's experience of daily life: it does. It enriches the world which is already present and adds great depth and beauty to the life one already leads. But this is all a re-affirmation of the world this present self already knows and understands -- the world of the first poem and not the second. For the first poem, whether present or absent, cised or non-cised, it is forms that establish and organize the perceptual field. "In seeking the ultimate enlightenment one will not succeed with such an understanding."

But how might one conceive of a world in which forms are not primary?

4.5 One Bright Pearl: Buddha Essence is Enlightenment

Understanding the work of emptiness as subtraction/essence yields quite a different reading of Dōgen's fascicles on enlightenment. Take, for example, the fascicle "One Bright Pearl" ("Ikka Myōju") which deals directly with the interpretation and expression of enlightenment. The fascicle revolves around Dōgen's interpretation of an exchange between Master and disciple where first one, then the other states: "The entire universe is one bright pearl. How do you understand this?"[225] Although commentators agree that Dōgen uses the pearl metaphor to express his understanding of enlightenment, there seems to be at least two possible interpretations of the nature of this understanding.

A reading which privileges affirmative co-dependent arising might see this fascicle as Dōgen's absolute affirmation of the conditioned world we all live in. The metaphor of "One Bright Pearl" is merged with "Indra's Net." One becomes a small pearl or jewel upon authenticating one's true self in the realization of one's co-dependent nature. One's own shining jewel is connected to and reflects the jewel-like mirrored nature of all others. As one scholar has put it:

> To use Dōgen's poetic image of the "one bright pearl," the world of conditioned co-arising is "one bright pearl" and each individual, by virtue of its relation to the whole, must also be "one bright pearl."[226]

The entire universe is then seen to be composed of an infinite number of interdependent bright jewels.

Dōgen, however, states that the universe is one bright pearl, and not an infinite number of bright pearls (as would be the case if there were an infinite number of interdependent bright pearl-jewels). In addition, the many phrases Dōgen uses to elaborate on "One bright pearl" do not seem to fit in this first reading. For example:

> This grass or that tree are not grass and tree, nor are the mountains and rivers of the world mountains and rivers; they are one bright pearl.[227]

Is every tree or mountain a pearl as well? Later in the fascicle Dōgen puts it even more strongly. He states:

> We do not speak of two or three pearls, and so the entirety is one True Dharma Eye, the Body of Reality, One Expression. The entirety is brilliant light, One Mind.[228]

A co-dependent arising reading does not seem adequate to account for these words of Dōgen.

A "Buddha essence" reading could see the fascicle as an attempt to set up a non-interdependent metaphor in order to shift monks from the first aspect of zazen to the second (from the conditioned to the non-conditioned, or in Tathāgatagarbha language, from "bees" to "honey"). The two different readings each depend on different views of the pearl. The co-dependent arising reading sees the pearl, or interconnected pearls, "out there": a never-ending, interconnected net of bright pearls. Since there is infinite interconnectedness, there is universal emptiness (emptiness in this case meaning empty of independent existence).

The Buddha essence reading might see the pearl from "within." In this case the pearl is so all-encompassing that it must include the reader as well: since no beginning or end is visible, there is infinite emptiness. A radical shift in perspectives is required to find one's enlightened nature. One's focus must completely change from entities (even if co-dependently arisen) to essence. In the fascicle Dōgen states:

> Do not be anxious about being reborn in one of the six realms of cause and effect. The bright pearl, which from beginning to end is essentially uninvolved [with cause and effect], is your original face, your enlightened nature.[229]

Enlightenment is somehow "uninvolved" with the conditioned realm. Later in the fascicle Dōgen continues with a statement reminiscent of the earlier quotation (on perspectival shifts) from "Genjōkōan":

> Because of the pursuing of things and making them the self the universe in its entirety is unceasing. And because its own nature is prior to such activity, it is beyond grasp even through the essence of the activity.
> One bright pearl is able to express Reality without naming it, and we can recognize this pearl as its name. One bright pearl communicates directly through all time; being through all the past unexhausted, it arrives through all the present.[230]

Again, the self's "own nature" is prior to conditioned activity.

It is possible to see the two readings (co-dependent arising and Buddha essence) as expressions of the two aspects of practice. From the perspective of the individual but interdependent self (the first aspect), we are all interconnected jewels in Indra's Net (the conventional truth of the conditioned realm; the first wisdom). The action of each individual jewel affects and is reflected in all other jewels. From the perspective of enlightenment (the second aspect), the Universe is "One Bright Pearl," boundless in nature and brilliance (the ultimate truth of the unconditioned realm; the second wisdom). However, with Dōgen, the first metaphor must be seen as incomplete, and the goal is to move to the second understanding of Buddha essence. While the second wisdom of emptiness (or the second aspect of practice) embraces the first, the first does not embrace the second. To reiterate: "because its own nature is prior to such activity, it is beyond grasp even through the essence of activity."[231]

The Buddha essence reading of Dōgen's "One Bright Pearl" can be further developed using the analogy of the wave/particle theory of light. Again, Dōgen states:

> We do not speak of two or three pearls, and so the entirety is one True Dharma Eye, the Body of Reality, One Expression. The entirety is brilliant light, One Mind.[232]

If "the entirety is brilliant light" is a description of Dōgen's emptiness, and light has both a particle and a wave nature, then seeing emptiness as having two natures may be helpful in understanding its behaviour.[233] Perhaps, Indra's Net is better visualized not only as a net of interconnected particle-selves but also as a wave of brilliant light. This wave of light is not static but moves, and exerts a "force" upon the particle-selves. The net as a whole then takes on the characteristics of the force (Buddha essence) of the larger wave. Wave, then, embraces particle, but particle does not embrace wave.

Seeing the net as light does not negate its particle nature, nor does seeing the light as a set of interconnected particles negate its wave nature -- once the action of the wave upon the particle is realized. Following this analogue through to the end, the goal of practice would then be to dwell in one's "particle-nature" while realizing that "wave-nature" is primary and governs behaviour. This requires not only a shift in focus from particle to wave but a shift in the mode of awareness that guides action, from particle sensitivities to wave sensitivities. This shift in sensitivities requires the subtraction of defilements before essence can be realized.

4.6 Essence and Ethics

A short exchange between Dōgen and a layman in the *Shōbōgenzō Zuimonki* can help begin to unfold the relationship I see between essence and ethics. The passage reads:

> A layman in the audience came up and asked: "Nowadays, when laymen give offerings to monks and take refuge in Buddhism, much misfortune is apt to result. They become prejudiced and do not wish to rely on the three treasures. What about this?"

> Dōgen answered: "This isn't the fault of the monks or of Buddhism, but it is the laymen themselves who are in error. This is why: you may respectfully make offerings to monks who seem to uphold the precepts, follow the eating regulations, and practice strict discipline; yet you do not give to monks who brazenly violate the precepts, drink wine, and eat meat because you consider them unworthy. A mind that discriminates in this way clearly violates the principles of Buddhism. Therefore, even if you take refuge in Buddhism, there is no merit and no response. The precepts contain several passages that caution against just this attitude.

When you meet a monk, make offerings to him, regardless of his virtue
or lack of it. By all means avoid trying to judge his inner virtue by his
outward appearance. . . .If you make offerings and show reverence
impartially, you will always be following the Buddha's will and will at
once gain benefits."[234]

Dōgen's response seems somewhat unusual. One might ask: Why should the layman
respect someone who does not deserve it? Is anger or disrespect not justified in a
situation in which someone abuses our trust?

Dōgen's response begins to makes sense when it is read through the two
aspects of practice. "Cutting the root of thinking" can be seen in relation to the
possible anger or distrust of the layman. The initial move in meditation might be
from "I am angry" to "anger is arising." The latter statement requires a coming to
terms with the conditioned nature of thoughts and images. The object of the anger
can no longer be foregrounded and an attempt is made instead to focus on emptiness.
"I am angry" is a vectored state which has an object, in this case the wine-drinking,
meat-eating monk. Emptiness, on the other hand, is vectorless. The problem (at
this stage) is not so much the presence of anger or distrust but the deliberate selection
of it: in choosing which course to take the lay person is focusing on defects rather
than virtues (of Buddha essence). By acting on thoughts of disrespect as they
arise, the Buddhist student steps out of the focus on emptiness and thus makes a
mistake in his or her own practice. Hence Dōgen's caution:"A mind that
discriminates in this way clearly violates the principles of Buddhism." This, I
think, is the emptiness and the practice of the novice monk. It is precisely the work
of "cutting the root of thinking."

But what about the second aspect of practice, dropping off body and mind?
How might the response of the Zen master be different? Although the practice of
meditation allows the novice monk access to a more intuitive mode of experiencing
the world, this intuitive state may still be distorted: responses such as anger, the
urge to criticize others or to be disrespectful continue to present themselves within
the meditative state. Over time, however, the nature of the thoughts and emotions
arising changes as defilements are subtracted. Just as one does not respond to
emotions of anger and disrespect in oneself, so one does not respond to these in
others, for in both cases this response reinforces false notions of self and existence.
There comes a time when, for at least one moment, the root of thinking is cut and
the barriers to a perspectival shift are removed. What is "primary" in orienting
perception shifts from defilements to essence. After this shift occurs, a different
sort of intuitive response may arise: one that responds not to the externals of the
situation (the monk violating the precepts, for example) but to the unconditioned

emptiness of the Buddha essence. One moves from the first aspect to the second by acting as if one were already in harmony with Buddha essence (or, in the example from the *Ratnagotra*, focusing on the "gold" rather than the "pebbles and sand"), gradually bringing together the immediate intuitive response with unconditioned emptiness.

Meditation works in the space between stimulus and response: it opens and explores the gap between thought and action. It is possible to think something without doing it. It is possible for a thought to arise without choosing to think about it further. In other words, one can choose to do other than that which presents itself. Although there is no control over instinctual responses in the short term, there is in the long term. It is through selecting a response other than, for example, the anger that is present that the anger is eventually "subtracted." By choosing to see anger as secondary, rather than primary, the initial instinctual response is no longer fueled and gradually changes.

This reading of Zen practice is one which perceives tension and difficulty in Dōgen's studying the way. The "gap" of zazen is the place of Dōgen's *gyōji* (continuous practice), -- the activity, effort or exertion involved in acting one way in the midst of forces and pressures (the five desires and the five hindrances) to act otherwise. The primary nature of force or affect is acknowledged and worked. This is the work of emptiness -- how emptiness is worked. *Gyōji* is "unremitting practice," or "conduct that continues constantly without stopping."[235]

Dōgen emphasizes the necessity of continuous practice both before and after realization. There is an edge that needs always to be worked in order to wear away "restraints" or "covers." Although Buddha essence is innate, it is not realized or visible without practice. In "Busshō" (Buddha Nature), Dōgen writes:

> The truth of the Buddha-nature is that the Buddha-nature is not endowed before actualizing a buddha, but endows itself after actualizing a buddha. The Buddha-nature and buddha-actualization always go simultaneously.[236]

Or, as Dōgen states in "Bendōwa":

> Although this Dharma inheres in each one of us in abundance, it does not become visible without practice, nor is it realized without enlightenment.[237]

Through this practice of sustained exertion the covers are burned off and the affective mode of the student gradually changes.[238] *Gyōji* is thus an ethical exertion that precedes the covers of the conditioned realm. Dōgen states:

It should be examined and understood thoroughly that dependent origination is *gyōji* but *gyōji* is not dependent origination."[239]

The work of essence precedes but does not deny, (co)dependent origination. In the same way, the Buddha essence reading of Dōgen does not deny (co)dependent arising; it just denies that it is primary or ultimate in Buddhist practice.

To return to the wave-particle analogy, wave embraces particle but particle does not embrace wave. While the "wave sense" (Buddha essence) of the second aspect of practice, or the second wisdom of emptiness, embraces the "particle logic" of the first, it is not the same as the logic of the first. These differing logics both lead to different understandings of meditation practice and have different implications for the relationship of Zen practice to karma. Dōgen's practice follows not the dialectical logic of (co)dependent arising but a logic of subtraction/essence. Following the practice of subtraction will eventually create the conditions necessary for a shift to an essence that precedes the conditioned realm. It is the "sense" of this preceding realm (essence), not (co)dependent arising, that guides Dōgen's writings and is the key to understanding the place of enlightenment in his thought. Dōgen's practice then pivots on this shift from the first realm to the second.

In my view, there are two serious mistakes one can make in reading Dōgen. First, one may read Dōgen through only the first aspect of practice and see the whole of practice as basically one of "cutting the root of thinking" through the removal of the five hindrances. One is progressively "purified" as defilements are eliminated. "Dropping off body and mind" is then a gradual process of purification. One sees the same way as one did before, only better, or more clearly. Practice is a gradual process of re-tuning the self.[240] In Tathāgatagarbha language, this might be the removal of the "sand and pebbles," but it is not the realization of the "gold." This is a dependent arising reading of Dōgen -- a Buddhism without enlightenment. Within Dōgen's writings, this reading seems incompatible with the radical shift in perspectives suggested by the quotations above.

Second, by collapsing "body and mind drop away" to the ordinary practice of meditation, one may read Dōgen through only the second stage of practice. "Body and mind drop away" is then reduced to a "whole body" realization of what one is able already to understand intellectually, that the self and all things are empty. The "sudden" move here is from "attachment" to "non-attachment." The images and affects that appear in the body and mind (including defilements) stay the same, but because one knows these "things" are empty, one is not attached to them. This is a co-dependent arising reading of Dōgen -- a Buddhism without karmic purification. (Again, the affirmative, dialectical logic of "is/is not" is incompatible with the subtraction or transformation of affective states such as anger.) Further, enlightenment can be accounted for only by reducing it to a state of non-attachment. This is the basic position of any number of scholars who read Buddhist meditation as an act of "presencing."

These above interpretations offer slightly different readings of the practice of meditation but do not adequately account for Dōgen's writings on enlightenment. They are unable to account for any significant shift in perception and understanding when "body and mind drop away" (enlightenment is reduced to meditation -- they must say that all meditation is "body and mind drop away"). As noted above, however, there is zazen before "body and mind drop away" and there is zazen "after" "body and mind drop away," but the affective content of these practices is not the same. How is it that, as Dōgen states, not all chief monks know true zazen? It is because "cutting the root of thinking" is not the same as "dropping off of body and mind."

What arises in the meditation of the monk is not the same as what arises in the meditation of the fourth stage Arahat -- while both share the same attitude towards that which arises (thoughts, images, affect, karma etc.), the affective nature of what arises is completely different. Further, and most important, the perceptual structure within which meditation practice occurs has changed radically from one defined and governed by defilements to one defined and governed by Buddha essence. This is the critical point -- there has been a radical shift in what is primary in the orientation of perception. (The whole of the next chapter is an attempt to address this one point.) Although the practice of zazen remains constant, the understanding of the emptiness which governs zazen undergoes a fundamental shift. The nature of this emptiness is now not a matter of thinking (or without thinking) but of desire and sense (or unsense -- essence). Dōgen's "dropping off of body and mind" is much more radical than a shift from thinking to without thinking, it is a shift in what is primary in organizing one's reality: a shift from an "unthought" to an "unsense" -- essence.

5 CONSTRUCTING A PHILOSOPHY OF ESSENCE: READING BUDDHISM THROUGH THE TWO NATURES OF DESIRE

> A thing has as many senses as there are forces capable of taking possession of it. But the thing itself is not neutral and will have more or less affinity with the force in current possession. There are forces which can only get a grip on something by giving it a restrictive sense and a negative value. Essence, on the other hand, will be defined as that one, among all the senses of a thing, which gives it the force with which it has the most affinity.
>
> -- Gilles Deleuze[241]

As noted in Chapter One, working with Chan/Zen texts is an activity that oscillates between "objectivity" and "imagination."[242] Acceptable readings of a text might be seen to exist on a continuum within these two limits: in the narrowest (and perhaps most "objective") sense, a reading is acceptable only if it can be consistently supported through direct reference to the text; in the broadest (and perhaps most "imaginative") sense, a reading is acceptable, and can be very creative, as long as it does not in any way contradict the text. Within these limits all readings must meet certain standards of consistency, comprehensiveness and explanatory power. While the leaning in the previous chapter was toward objectivity (in continually documenting textual sources to support the argument), the leaning in this chapter is toward imagination. It is a creative interpretation and appropriation of Dōgen, an attempt to remain consistent with the grain of Dōgen's thought while extending it further with reference to desire and affect.

My claim is that Buddhist practice is best presented not as a move from one form of thinking to another (from thinking to without thinking) but as a move from one nature of desire to another (from craving to compassion). What distinguishes the third reading from the first two is that Buddhist emptiness is not seen as an achieved state of thinking but as an achieved state of desire.

Understanding emptiness in this way requires a different reading of Buddhism, one which sees the nature and function of desire and affect as primary in Buddhist practice.

Two obstacles have to be overcome in an attempt to construct a comprehensive Buddhist position based in desire and affect, what I am calling a Buddhism of essence. The first obstacle is karma: how to account for Dōgen's "removal of the five defilements"? If these are subtracted in meditation, how does this occur and what does it mean? The second obstacle is "dropping off body and mind." This is unquestionably an important point in Dōgen's writings, but, again, how does one understand this phrase? Understanding "dropping off body and mind" is especially problematic if this is an event or realization distinct from the mature practice of meditation, "cutting the root of thinking." Another way to put this problem might be: How does one distinguish between two senior monks, one who has had a "realization of emptiness" and one who has not? If there are such experiences, how might they occur and what might they mean?

My own attempt to overcome these two interpretive obstacles centers on further opening up the distinction between Dōgen's two aspects of studying the way, "cutting the root of thinking" and "dropping off body and mind." Again, Dōgen states that one studies the way . . .

> . . . by sitting, which severs the root of thinking and blocks access to the road of intellectual understanding. This is an excellent means to arouse true beginner's mind. Then you let body and mind drop away and let go of delusion and enlightenment. This is the second aspect of studying the way.
>
> Generally speaking, those who trust that they are within the buddha way are most rare. If you have correct trust that you are within the buddha way, you understand where the great way leads or ends, and you know the original source of delusion and enlightenment. If once, in sitting, you sever the root of thinking, in eight or nine cases out of ten you will immediately attain understanding of the way.[243]

I suggest that the two aspects of practice represent two distinctly different perceptual fields and that the nature of desire in the second field is quite different from that of the first. The work of emptiness is then not the work of presence or difference in thinking, but the work of essence in sense, desire and affect.

5.1 Desire and Affect

Though cessation of desire is usually seen as the concern in Buddhism, my claim is that the issue is really the transformation of desire. My position is that thinking and perception cannot be separated from desire and affect, and that the key to the cultivation and maintenance of a perceptual field in which emptiness, not form, is primary lies in working with desire or affect. This transformed perceptual field might then be accompanied by, and dependent on, a transformed affective mode -- again, an affective mode in which form is not primary.

The Japanese use of *ai* offers two ways to think about desire. The same root term "*ai*" can be taken in completely different directions: one is "defiled" desire -- lust and craving; the other is "undefiled" desire -- selfless compassion.

> *Ai*: Love [or Desire]. Broadly speaking, Buddhism recognizes two kinds of *ai*; the first is *ai* stemming from attachment to self and includes desire for fame wealth, and carnal pleasure; the second kind of *ai* is that of the Buddhas and *bodhisattvas* and is characterized by selfless compassion for all beings. The former is called defiled love [or desire] (*zemma-ai*) and the latter undefiled love [or desire] (*fuzemma-ai*).
> *Aigo*: Kind words, affectionate words. One of the four virtues of the *bodhisattvas*.
> *Aiketsu*: The bondage of craving. One of the nine fetters of defilement.
> *Aiyoku*: Passion. Lust. Lust and desire. Love and desire. Love of family. Also called the stream of love, the ocean of desire, the poison of lust, etc.[244]

Lust and compassion, then, share a common source; though different in nature they are not different in kind. (Neither is an Other.) But if forms are not primary, what is? -- perhaps selfless compassion. The first perceptual field is the field of defiled desire, while the second is the field of undefiled desire. Buddhist emptiness might then be that state achieved when the field of defiled love or desire gives way to the field of selfless compassion.

Re-working the word "defilement" may help clarify this line of thinking. There are a number of Sanskrit words translated into English as "defilement," the main one being *kleśa*. But one of the other lesser-used Sanskrit terms, *āsrava*, allows for a rendering other than "defilement." According to Jikido Takasaki, *āsrava* literally means "having outflows" or "having leaks."[245] *Anāsrava* is then "without outflows" and *anāsrava-dhātu* (used to describe nirvana) is then the "realm without outflows."

Following from this understanding of "defilement" as "outflows," Buddhist practice can be read as encouraging a move from the realm of outflows to the realm without outflows. This is done by the maintaining a practice of "no outflowing." To put it another way, one lets go of states of mind which "leak," or "stream," so that the intensity of desire can increase and the positive qualities of the "non-streaming" state of mind can manifest themselves.

The work of Gilles Deleuze on desire is helpful in providing a way of conceiving of these two natures of desire. Along with Felix Guattari, he articulates a series of splits, choices, intersections and decision points at which one must choose between one form of desire and another.[246] These choices or directions can be described as follows:

i. There is a choice between life lived as a climax-being or life lived as a plateau-being. A plateau is defined as "a continuous, self-vibrating region of intensities whose development avoids any orientation toward a culmination point or external end."[247]

ii. The choice between climax and plateau is also a choice between two kinds of desire -- one chooses either to pursue pleasure/discharge or to maintain the intensity of positive desire. Deleuze's main metaphor here seems to be the sex act itself and the conflict that exists between pursuing the pleasure of climax and maintaining the intensity of the plateau of desire.[248] (Other examples of pursuing pleasure/discharge would be acts of anger, war and fear.)[249]

iii. The choice between climax and plateau is also a choice between becoming more of what we already are (which Deleuze calls becoming being) or moving in a direction where we become something new (which Deleuze calls becoming becoming). Both are a process, but the former is a process of intensifying the present state of being while the latter is a process in which one becomes something other.

In order to distinguish between the two uses of *ai*, I will use the word "pleasure" to mean desire-as-lack and the seeking of pleasure, and retain the term "desire" for the desire of becoming and the maintenance of the plateau of intensity. Pleasure and desire then exist on different lines: one on the line of being and one on the line of becoming. In a sense both are lines of becoming, but one is a line of becoming more of the same and one is a line of becoming other. One is the line of the possible and one is a line that leads outside the realm of the possible into the realm of the potential. "Possibility is a restricted range of potential: what the thing can become without ceasing to be itself (how the process can end without ending up outside)."[250] This is also the difference between the question, "What can it do without ceasing to be itself?" and the question "How is it forever becoming other than it is?"[251] The line of pleasure and the line of desire are always intersecting in our bodies and this intersection is always taking place in the present moment in that space between stimulus and response. Choosing pleasure over desire is then simultaneously choosing being over becoming, climax over plateau, and the possible over the potential.

To make the link to Buddhism explicit: the move from the realm of the possible to the realm of the potential is understood as a shift from the first aspect of practice to the second; from sensitivity to forms and pleasures to sensitivity to essence and positive desire (from sense to essence). The space between stimulus and response (where the line of pleasure and the line of desire intersect) is the location of Buddhist meditation practice. If we wish to change the direction of becoming, then we must work with all the possibilities which arise in that gap.

In Deleuze's language, we can continue to progress toward being more of what we already are, or choose otherwise -- to think and act other than we have in the past. Put differently, we can move to re-establish the self by choosing pleasure, or we can allow the self to be broken down by maintaining the state of positive desire.

I think it is a matter of coding. Operating out of instinctual codes leads to the seeking of pleasure. Following the line of desire goes against instinctual codes and may result in pain. One of the consequences of choosing to maintain the plateau of desire is to burn away any instinctual codes which promote the seeking of pleasure. Clearly this is not a joy-producing task in all its stages, for it is only when the pleasure-seeking instinctual codes are burned away that the joy of the line of desire may be experienced. Burning away these instinctual codes is the precondition for moving outside the realm of the possible and into the realm of the potential.

This is where the Buddhist understanding of karma comes in. We have no control over our instinctual or coded responses in the short term but we do in the long term (through meditation practice). Natural thought, or initial instinctual response (karmic response), depends upon actions previously taken, actions which could have been otherwise. It is by choosing to act otherwise that we burn off the instinctual codes or dissolve karmic hindrances and defilements (outflowing tendencies).

When one works the possibilities in the gap between stimulus and response, the gap is transformed into a space of becoming. The strict correspondence between what we are and the ideas, opinions and emotions that occur within us breaks down. We can choose to do other than that which presents itself. It is possible for a thought to arise without choosing to think about it further. It is also possible to think something without doing it. The becoming self is not dependent on what this present body thinks, feels or understands.

The problem is one of choice. How to distinguish between pleasure and positive desire, between that which needs to burn away and that which can be pursued? What karmic blocks or defilements are to be subtracted, dissolved or transformed, and to what end? Any attempt to address the question of ethics must begin: How to choose?

5.2 Recoding Desire: The Work of Buddha Essence

In an "ethics of desire," pleasure is always the unethical choice. Pleasure is cised and vectored (defiled or outflowing): desire is non-cised and non-vectored (without outflows). If one wishes to pursue the line of becoming, then one must choose against cised and vectored responses. The present moment allows both possibilities, but only consistency in the choice of the non-cised possibilities leads outside and beyond the present instinctual coding and into the realm of the potential (through the dissolution of karmic defilements or outflowing tendencies).

The difficulty is that one can know little about the realm of the potential (Buddha essence) from the perspective of the realm of the possible (one's present state of coding: sensitivity to forms), because the realm of the potential lies outside present coding and thinking. We can only ever use our present state of thinking (the possible) to think about what we cannot now think (the potential). The move from the possible to the potential (from forms, pleasures and defilements to positive desire and essence) requires decoding (again, burning off karma or dissolving defilements) and recoding. Changes in coding must precede knowledge of the realm of the potential as present knowledge is always governed by dominant codes.[252] Or, to return to Dōgen's two aspects of studying the way, cutting the root of thinking must precede dropping off body and mind; burning off defilements must precede realization of Buddha essence. "Subtraction" is a "burning off" of outflowing tendencies which can occur only with a sustained increase in the positive desire of the field.

The appearance a particular choice takes on would depend on the nature of the specific codes at work at the moment the choice is made. Since decoding and recoding are taking place all the time, the same action may be understood differently at different times. In the perceptual field where form is primary, the choice of pleasure over desire may appear to be a move which enriches and satisfies; in the opposed perceptual field, where form is not primary, the same choice can appear as a simplification and a reduction in the intensity of desire. We must, then, distinguish between intensities of desire and intensities of pleasure, knowing that one can flip to the other in the blink of an eye. There is consistency in understanding only through commitment to a particular direction: toward pleasure or desire, toward being or becoming, towards forms or essence. Each is a process, but they move in different directions. Consistency in moving toward essence is what marks Buddhist practice.

The choice to pursue pleasure (forms) is a fall from, or collapse of, the plateau of non-streaming positive desire (essence). If pleasure-decoding has not taken place, any increasing intensity of desire is experienced not as bliss or joy but as pain: if the pain cannot be tolerated, then one chooses to lessen the intensity by discharging desire along an escape vector (an "outflow" or "defilement"). Before the intensity can be experienced as joyful, the pleasure-seeking instinctual coding must be modified. Again, in Buddhist language, karma must be burned off or defilements purified before the nature and experience of desire significantly changes. When pleasure-decoding has taken place (when escape vectors have dissolved or been subtracted), desire may be experienced more intensely and with greater duration and joy, thus creating new non-vectored codes.[253]

5.3 Desire, Figure and Ground: Cultivating Field Sensitivities

The concepts of field dependent and field independent perceptual fields, borrowed from the psychology of perception, are useful in this context. One of the classic tests for field dependence/independence is the "embedded figures test." How easy is it for a person to abstract a figure from an ambiguous background? Those able to do this easily tend toward the field independent end of the spectrum. Those who cannot do this, or who do so with difficulty, tend toward the field dependent end. The simplistic generalization is that hunters tend toward the field independent in their ability to abstract game from an ambiguous background, while farmers tend toward the field dependent in that their work does not require highly developed skills in perceptual abstraction.

Field independence is considered normative. As such, there is little evidence of a corresponding positive test to measure field dependence (i.e. to measure degree of sensitivity to the field rather than simply relying on the negative measure of lack of sensitivity to the figure). In modifying these terms (for use in this chapter) I would like to suggest an expanded understanding of field dependence where field dependent persons demonstrate a greater sensitivity to the force or intensities of the field rather than to forms or figures.[254] Field dependent persons may have difficulty distinguishing a figure or design from a background because their sensitivities lie elsewhere. For example, in the previous hunter/farmer example, one might expect farmers to have greater sensitivity to atmospheric conditions of warmth, cold, light, moisture, etc.[255] An example of contrasting field sensitivities is reflected in the non-cised Impressionist paintings such as Monet's series of haystacks or cathedrals (which reflect field dependent sensitivities) and cised Expressionist paintings such as Van Gogh's series of shoes (which reflect field independent sensitivities).[256]

Field dependence, understood in this modified positive way, is helpful in understanding Buddhist meditation. The practice of meditation might be seen as a reverse embedded figure test: a measure of how well one does in choosing the field rather than abstracting the figure. Or, put differently, the figure dominating meditation is already abstracted from the field and the test is to choose the field in the presence of the figure. In meditation, however, this figure or image is not a neutral embedded number or geometric shape: the image comes with vectors of force. Buddhist practice requires a decoding and a recoding: a loss in sensitivity to the force and specificity of figure-differences and a gain in sensitivity to the field-forces that sustain the differences.[257]

Deleuze and Guattari's discussion of striated space and smooth space helps further articulate the difference between the two perceptual fields. Field independence (figure sensitivity) is striated space perception. Field dependent perception is smooth space perception -- what might be Deleuze and Guattari's "Eskimo space."[258]

> Where there is close vision, space is not visual, or rather the eye itself has a haptic, nonoptical function: no line separates earth from sky, which are of the same substance; there is neither horizon nor background nor perspective nor limit nor outline or form nor center; there is no intermediary distance, or all distance is intermediary. Like Eskimo space.[259]

In the move from figure to field sensitivities, or from the striated to the smooth, perception shifts from the optical to the tactile. Or perhaps "haptic" is a better word than "tactile," as it "invites the assumption that the eye itself may fulfil this nonoptical function."[260]

Field independent (figure-directed, figure-sensitive) experience must of necessity be of limited intensity, because the coding that it requires is not set up to sustain intensities but to discharge them. As the intensity of desire increases, one of two things must happen: either desire is discharged through a vector (again, vector and defilement are synonymous), thus further re-affirming any already existing pleasure-seeking codes in the figure-sensitive perceptual structure; or the pleasure-seeking coding begins to be burned away (karmic defilements are purified) and the beginnings of the move to field sensitivities (recoding) becomes possible. The modification of the coding, or the cultivation of different sorts of sensitivities, occurs with the maintenance of smooth space and haptic vision. With this shift in awareness and sensitivities from the optic to the haptic comes the ability to withstand increased intensities of desire, and with this increase (and the simultaneous recoding) comes a change in the nature and experience of desire.

Deleuze presents an example of a perceptual field in which form is not primary in his article "Michel Tournier and the World without Others."[261] Deleuze draws from Michel Tournier's book *Friday*,[262] a redoing of the Robinson Crusoe story, to examine how our relationship to objects is developed and maintained. He suggests perception may occur within two different worlds: a "structure-other" world and an "elemental" world -- a world without others.

Deleuze's Other is not an object in the perceptual field but that which makes the (structure-other) perceptual field possible in the first place. This Other is then an "a priori Other" which establishes the field independent perceptual framework within which actual subject-others can exist. Deleuze writes:

> But the Other is neither an object in the field of my perception nor a subject who perceives me: the Other is initially a structure of the perceptual field without which the entire field could not function as it does. . . . Thus the a priori Other, as the absolute structure, establishes the relativity of others as terms actualizing the structure within each field.

> We must understand that the Other is not one structure among others in the field of perception (in the sense, for example, that one would recognize in it a difference of nature from objects). It is the structure which conditions the entire field and its functioning by rendering possible the constitution and application of the preceding categories. It is not the ego but the Other as structure which renders perception possible.[264]

This suggests that another way of perceiving is possible in a "world without Others." Again, the "world without Others" has nothing to do with the presence or absence of actual others, but with the dissolution of the field independent perceptual framework necessary to posit others as distinct embodied images requiring focused attention. In Tournier's Crusoe tale, the absence of others on the island is extremely disturbing to Robinson. Deleuze writes:

> The structure-Other organizes and pacifies depth. It renders it livable. This is why the agitations of this structure imply a disorder, a disturbance of depth, as an aggressive return of the bottomless abyss that can no longer be conjured away. Everything has lost its sense. . . unless he [Robinson] invents a new dimension or a third sense for the

expression "loss of Others"; unless the absence of the Other and the dissolution of its structure do not simply disorganize the world but, on the contrary, open up a possibility of salvation. Robinson must return to the world of surface and discover surfaces. The pure surface is perhaps what Others were hiding from us. It is perhaps at the surface, like a mist, that an unknown image of things is detached and, from the earth, a new surface energy without possible others.[265]

When the field independent structure-Other framework dissolves, an elemental luminosity appears. This elemental luminosity is lost in the structure-Other framework because of the tension required to structure and focus cised and vectored figure-sensitive perception.

Deleuze suggests that the term "dualism," traditionally used to describe the subject-other relationship in the first perceptual field, needs to be rethought and redefined. He writes:

> . . . we doubt that dualism is correctly defined as long as it is established between the matter of the perceptual field and the pre-reflective syntheses of the ego. The true dualism lies elsewhere; it lies between the effects of the "structure Other" of the perceptual field and the effects of its absence (what perception would be were there no Others).[266]

Dualism should really refer to the difference between the two perceptual fields.

When Deleuze's distinction between the two perceptual fields is coupled with the concepts of field dependence/independence, it becomes possible to see a much more radical difference between the two poems in the legend of the Sixth Patriarch. The cultivation of field sensitivities might be seen as a starting point in the movement towards a "perception without others" and may be useful in attempting to understand the perceptual field of the second poem: a vision where form is not primary. Again, the two poems are:

Shen Hsiu: The body is the Bodhi tree,
              The mind is like a clear mirror.
              At all times we must strive to polish it,
              And must not let the dust collect.

Hui Neng: Bodhi originally has no tree,
              The mirror also has no stand.
              From the beginning not a thing is,
              Where is there room for dust?[267]

It is not that the perceptual framework stays the same, but is emptied; it is that the perceptual framework required for forms to be primary dissolves. The second poem is not about forms at all, for even empty forms require the structure-Other perceptual framework. There has been a decoding and a recoding. The second poem may be written to describe "what perception would be like if there were no Others" -- the "elemental luminosity" of a "world without others."

Buddhist practice would then not be about changing one's relationship to what appears to be (so the thing is experienced directly rather than through the dust of opinions and concepts), nor would it be about changing one's understanding of things as they appear to be (so these things are understood to be not independent but relative and interdependent), rather it would be about changing the field of the "appears to be" altogether, so that what is primary is no longer a field of "things" at all. The perceptual/thinking structure changes completely through the cultivation and privileging of different sensitivities. It is this sustained increase in the "elemental luminosity" of the field that the vision of the first poem can never see, and that the instinctual codes underlying the first poem can never tolerate. Forms are no longer primary.

5.4 Thinking and Essence: Difference and Desire

But what is the place of thinking in a perceptual field where forms are not primary? The relationship of thinking to essence can be approached by examining the relationship between difference and desire. The nothing/gap/difference might be seen as the relation between thoughts: the gap that separates as well as joins thoughts.[268] Difference is the gap between thoughts which allows thinking to function but cannot itself be thought.[269] But terms such as gap or between are problematic. The "nothing" is not only the gap between thoughts but also the relation of one thought to another and the medium in which that relation occurs. For example, the thought "horse" is not pure "horse" but also contains a trace of the thought "not cow." There is a necessary gap between the thought "horse" and the thought "not cow." There must be a between (difference, gap, nothing) that relates one thought to the next. As Rodolphe Gasché has put it, there are. . .

> . . . blanks between the marks that relate the marks to each other. . . .the
> nature "proper" of the mark also demands that it refer to that which
> opens up the possibility of marks in general. . . . the seme mark is thus
> made to refer to its asemic space of inscription. . . . Derrida calls this
> space the mark's spaced out semiopening (l'entr'ouverture espacée).[270]

Any one thought actually contains traces of a number of thoughts that play with and against each other by virtue of a between. The nature of the relationship between thoughts is dependent on the nature of the gap between thoughts, for the gap is that which relates one thought to the next. "Each mark . . . must take on the fold of the asemic space that unfolds between the terms of the series or system."[271] Like any one image in a movie (at the usual 24 frames per second), any one thought embraces a number of thoughts and a number of gaps. In Gasché's terms, if "supplementarity, *différance* and arche-trace" all work by "establishing an Other, a double opposite to them,"[272] then this also establishes a necessary gap between the two components of the double. Heidegger and Taylor draw this gap differently, the former as presence (. . .) the latter as difference (the unending vertical o o o).

But what if this difference/gap/interval/between/blank is also the location of desire, drives, instinct or karma? What about the forces at work in this between? Of course, these forces can never be thought directly. If one is consciously thinking of one of these forces, it is as part of the chain of thoughts and not as part of the between. Perhaps, then, forces or karmic traces exist more as "ghosts" in the between, there and not there -- present, but always eluding the thinking process.

This yields both traces in each thought and ghosts in each between; the between is then the space in which the ghosts play out their existence. In thinking "horse" there is then not only the trace of "not cow" but also the force of the existence of the ghosts of the gap or between. The affective nature of the gap is then dependent on the nature of the ghosts (karmic traces) that inhabit it and it is these ghosts that relate one thought to the next. It is through inhabiting this medium of relation that these ghosts colour perception and thinking and regulate decision-making.

The Buddhist practice of meditation could then be seen as the practice of dredging the nothing -- the gap/abyss/nothing/between stimulus and response. This is the place(s) where the line of pleasure and line of desire intersect, the habitus of the ghosts. It is by developing a sensitivity to this "between" in meditation practice that the "between" begins to relax or open. Following this relaxation some of the ghosts which infect thinking escape to consciousness (in meditative practice) thus altering the content and the affective nature of the between. To put it another way, the between, and that which inhabits the between, are held in place in state of tension by field independent forces. When these field independent forces begin to decrease in intensity and dissolve, that which was imprisoned in the between is released. The between is then no longer the same as it was: the affective nature of the medium of relation has changed. It is now less field independent (less figure sensitive) and more field sensitive. The ratio between defiled and non-defiled forces has changed.

The ghosts of the between make their presence known indirectly through figure-centered vectors of force: fear, desire-as-lack, anger. In Buddhist practice there are two forces at work in the gap: the pressure of the ghosts of the between to discharge at something and the exertion of zazen (*gyōji*) to maintain the intensity and luminosity of the field in the face of these field independent forces. This, though, is a double bind.[274] The Buddhist choice in this double bind is clear, but initially may be agonizing: to choose consistently to relate to the figure through relating to the field (for in this thinking the figure is of the field) against the pressure to abstract the figure from the field (and therefore reinforce the field independent vectors/coding/perceptual structure). Making this choice has both short-term and long-term consequences. In the short term it temporarily suspends the affects/ effects of the ghosts of the between on any single action. In the long term (i.e. when a similar choice is made consistently over time), it allows individual ghosts to arise in zazen and dissolve in the field, thus changing the content of the between and the nature of any force which pressures, organizes (and in some cases defines) future thinking. (It would seem quite possible to burn off or dissolve the force of the ghosts, and thus eventually the ghosts themselves, without conscious awareness of the "identity" of these ghosts. The point is important as it suggests that intellectual understanding is not crucial to the process.)

The practice of meditation works in two ways: first, the field independent (figure sensitive, figure directed) forces that are present are allowed to arise and dissolve (karma is burned off; defilements are purified), thus changing both the nature of and ratio between the forces at work in the gap/nothing; and second, there is the cultivation of an increased sensitivity to field dependent forces, giving those forces an increased power even when they are not dominant. From the perspective of Buddha essence, Buddhist practice is not an all-or-nothing situation where all karmic forces need to dissolve before enlightened choices can be made. One can choose to make field dependent forces primary in decision-making even when they are not dominant -- it is just harder. In these moments one needs to choose against the force that is present. Working against this grain in daily life makes Buddhist practice work. This is the work of emptiness as essence.

5.5 Dropping off Body and Mind

Returning to Dōgen's arahat, from the fascicle "A Monk at the Fourth Stage of Meditation," the monk in the story realized that he had not attained the fourth stage of meditation when he became fearful and angry. There are two points of note: first, the monk made the non-Buddhist choice to <u>be</u> angry; second, and more important, the monk had not reached the stage where the nature of the "between" had changed. Fear and anger are vectored affective states that arise in response to external circumstances: they stream or flow out. Through fear and anger the monk experiences outflowing desire and knows he is not, after all, an arahat, for outflowing desire requires a perceptual structure of otherness and difference that is not a part of the perception of the arahat. Outflowing desire is not a sin but simply a negative result in a check or test for the presence of the arahat's realm, a realm without outflows (*anāsrava-dhātu*). When the monk found himself acting upon these forces, he knew his experience was still regulated by karmic defilements (field independent, figure sensitive forces), and therefore structured in a perceptual system where form was still primary, a structure incompatible with the fourth stage of meditation.

Each of the monks understood that one of the marks of the fourth stage of meditation is that the nature of the desire that arises is not related to, or dependent on, forms or objects.[275]   This marks the difference between the two kinds of *ai* (desire), -- the *ai* which stems from attachment to self (which I have called pleasure) and the *ai* of the Buddhas and bodhisattvas (which I have called desire or essence). In the latter case, desire still exists, but in a non-vectored state: there is no object, no sexual "gaze" which both objectifies and consumes.[276]

This desire of the fourth stage of meditation, however, is not the same desire in a non-vectored state (which would, in principle, be impossible), but a desire that has changed its very nature in changing its state. In maintaining the non-vectored response, desire becomes more intense and burns off karmic defilements (affective escape vectors). Thus as desire becomes more intense, it changes its nature -- it is no longer figure-sensitive and vectored, but field sensitive and non-vectored (or radiant).

Buddhist practice then is the effort not to create or pursue (and thus re-affirm) the figure sensitive/figure directed affective vectors which appear especially attractive during those times of intense force (e.g. desire-as-lack, despair, anger, fear). In other words, the aim of Buddhist practice is not only to burn off karma, but not to create karma. The difficulty is in choosing to continue to dwell in this state of intense force (and even to allow it to increase in intensity) without acting to reduce intensity by "streaming out" along any of the escape vectors that suggest themselves. Any such streaming out only increases the strength of pleasure-coding and the presence of figure-directed vectors. These affective vectors act as guy-wires: they anchor the figure-sensitive perceptual structure and prevent the implosion of figure-sensitive subjectivity. It is through the continuing practice of acting other than one thinks/feels (the effort to not re-affirm vectors of force) that the guy-wires dissolve one by one, and the complex relationship between force and thinking that constitutes subjectivity turns inside out. There is a shift in what is primary from field independent forms (and their associated forces) to field sensitive force.

This "turning inside-out" is my reading of Dōgen's "dropping off of body and mind." Again, I see meditation as the process by which some ghosts of the between come to consciousness and dissolve, thus indirectly changing the nature of the process by which things come to representation. As the nature of the between (which is also a medium) loosens and becomes more flexible, it will eventually turn inside out, if only for a moment, reversing the relationship between thinking and affect, form and emptiness. The dissolution of some of the forces of the between allows its function as a medium to take precedence over its function as a between. This moment is a sudden switch and marks the first time field sensitive forces become primary in the representational process.[277] It is not that the differential structure (the field independent perceptual system) has been negated: it has simply turned inside out and is no longer primary. This could be likened to a figure/ground switch, but of the entire field, where the components are form and affect (rather than faces and goblet) and the shift is regulated by the transformation of force.

One way to describe the nature of this field of positive desire might be to use the term compassion. Compassion used in this sense, however, must not be misunderstood as yet another vectored force. In other words, it cannot be seen to depend on the presence or absence of specific persons or external conditions -- an Other calling for compassion. Compassion as dependent or contingent would be just another field independent force to be burned off or subtracted (similar to anger). (Joy, reverence and other positive terms used to describe this unconditioned realm would have to be understood as non-vectored as well.)

This field of positive non-cised desire is not a permanent and unchanging state, however, as the forces of the field/gap continue to fluctuate. The occurrence of this switch does not prevent the occasional dominance of field independent force. This switching back and forth is the continuing double-bind of meditation practice, especially in the early years after the initial insight. In order to be faithful to the initial realization the student must continue to choose to decide on the basis of field sensitivity even when figure sensitive forces are overwhelmingly dominant. Or, to put it another way, the student must continue to "translate" and act from the "inside-out" even when things are seen from the "outside-in."[278] When "dropping off body and mind" is understood in this way, it would be followed by a period of deepening insight (into the use of the new perceptual field) as the field independent forces continue to dissolve and field sensitivity continues to increase.

Although difference and desire are inextricably mixed, only one can act as a "transcendental" which structures perception and action (only one can be primary): the field of positive desire is the inside-out of the structure of difference. As one can experience desire in the midst of difference, so one can experience difference in the midst of desire: for a Buddhism of essence, however, difference cannot be primary in decision-making.

The crucial point to be made here is that only the work of subtraction (not negation) can lead to the turning-inside-out, the perspectival shift from the logic of an unthought to the sense of unsense. It is this unsense that is the essence of Dōgen's Buddhism.[279] Essence precedes sense similar to the way the unthought, or without thinking, precedes thought. There are two fields of force and desire -- one figure-sensitive, vectored and defiled (sense) and one field-sensitive, radiant and undefiled (essence). Sense is external to essence, external to the true self. Sense is part of the conditioned realm in that it is dependent on, or affected by, the presence or absence of external conditions (it is vectored). Essence is another name for the unconditioned realm, the realm that does not respond to the presence or absence of external conditions. To press the difference between sense and essence: anger arises in response to external conditions and must be subtracted as it is part of the conditioned realm, a form of sense; compassion is of the realm of no-outflows, independent of external conditions, a quality of essence. In my reading of Dōgen's Buddhism, working emptiness means making essence primary.

"Dropping off body and mind" then requires not only a shift from one governing unthought to another, but in the very nature of the unthought: a shift from the realm preceding thinking to the realm preceding sense. Clearly, this transverse shift is not only from thinking to non-thinking, or even from thinking to pure sense experience (from mind to body). Instead, it is from the realm of thought to the realm of the unsense, essence: dropping off mind (thinking) and body (sense).

Thomas Cleary is among those who tend toward this reading of Zen Buddhism in general, and Dōgen in particular. In an introduction to a translation of fascicles from the *Shōbōgenzō*, Cleary quotes from Sōzan:

> As a beginner, knowing there is something fundamental in oneself, when one turns the light around (shifts attention from sense to the essence of mind) one ejects form, sound, smell, flavor, touch, and phenomena, and attains tranquility. Then, after fully accomplishing this, one does not grasp the sense data but descends among them without being blinded, letting them be without interference.[280]

In Cleary's reading of Zen Buddhist practice one "shifts attention from sense to the essence of mind."

Later in his introduction Cleary uses a quotation from Dōgen which makes a similar point about the relationship between sense and essence:

> The *zazen* of the Buddhas is not motion or stillness, not practice or
> realization. . . . It doesn't empty mental objects, it doesn't cling to any
> realm of sense. . . . Study of the Way doesn't use form, sensation,
> conception, conditionings, or discriminating consciousness -- if you act
> on form, sensation, conception, conditionings, or discriminating
> consciousness, this is form, sensation, conception, conditions, and
> discriminating consciousness, not study of the Way.[281]

Again, the split is between sense and essence, the conditioned and the unconditioned
realm. Study of the way involves acting from the latter realm.

Re-reading "dropping off body and mind" as the move from the field of
sense (defiled desire) to the field of essence (an intense plateau of undefiled desire)
also requires a re-reading of Dōgen's metaphors of enlightenment. Dōgen's "One
Bright Pearl" is not a brilliant object that can be abstracted from the field but rather
a metaphorical description of the luminosity and intensity of the field as a whole.
As Kim translates, "the world of all the ten directions is one luminous pearl."[282]
The titles of other fascicles in the *Shōbōgenzō* can also be understood as descriptions
of the field: "Kōmyō" (radiant or dazzling light) and "Kokū" (universal emptiness).
Dōgen's classic shift from "all beings have Buddha Nature" to "whole being is
Buddha Nature" can also be read as a switch from figure to field sensitivities.
Buddha Nature is <u>not</u> a property of the figure within the field (the self is empty) but
rather is the radiant and luminous force of the field itself (emptiness is the self).
The "self" is re-located from figure to field.

Decision-making in the realm of essence would seem to require a "binocular
vision,"[283] maintaining essence (field-sense) as primary while working with
difference. In the position being presented here, the "Buddhist" choice is to decide
from one while acting in the other. This would be possible because the two realms
intersect rather than conflict; they exist in different dimensions. Enlightened practice
is the ability to deal with forms while at the same time maintaining the affective
intensity and elemental luminosity of the force of the field. The luminosity of the
field is constructed and maintained through the non-pursuit of vectors of force.
The price of pursuing the vectors of force which connect "objects" in the field is a
loss of the intense luminosity of the field.

From this perspective the only "mistake" is deliberately channeling the force
of the field down field independent figure-directed vectors or defilements. For
example, the choice to <u>be</u> angry is the deliberate decision to make forms primary
and negate the brilliance and intensity of the field, a choice that would be so
incomprehensible (to those within the field) that the only explanation can be that
the person involved must not be dwelling in elemental luminosity of the field (i.e.

Dōgen's fourth stage of meditation). He or she must still be governed by field independent figure-sensitive coding (karmic defilements). Further, focusing attention on figures abstracted from the field only serves to reinforce figure-sensitive coding and block the switch to (or maintenance of) a field-sensitive perception where form is not primary. Either of these practices would prevent the shift from the first aspect of practice to the second.

Maintaining the primacy (intensity, luminosity, radiance) of this essence would be the basis of an "ethics of essence."[284] This requires seeing the practice of Buddhism as one of deciding not to create vectors of force (defilements). As William Grosnick states,

> . . . it would seem that if one thought of practice not as the extinction of kleśas, but as the nonorigination of kleśas, practice would be endless, and would never bring one to any sort of final state. Backsliding would either always remain a possibility, or else it would remain a possibility as long as one had the mistaken idea that at some point in time one's kleśas would be extinct (then, conceivably one might erroneously relax his [or her] vigilance).[285]

It is, by (my) definition true that all field independent (figure sensitive, figure directed) forces are karmic defilements to be dissolved because they subtract from the nature and intensity of the desire of the field. The field-sensitive structure puts into question every figure-directed vector of force.[286] While there are two natures of desire -- defiled (outflowing) and undefiled (non-outflowing) -- the latter is primary in Buddhist thought and practice. The line of resistance in, and foundation of, a Buddhist ethics of desire is the wish to maintain the intensity and luminosity of the non-leaking realm.

6 DISTILLATIONS

The entire universe is one bright pearl. How do you understand this?
                                                                    -- Dōgen

How might Dōgen's "one bright pearl" look from the perspectives of the three readings of emptiness? And how might this matter?

The first understanding of the meaning of emptiness is as <u>co</u>-dependent arising. Emptiness here is emptiness of independent existence. Dōgen's "bright pearl" is the self when attachment to independent existence has dropped away. In the understanding of emptiness as co-dependent arising, there is no individual existence, or individual identity, but there <u>is</u> mutual existence or mutual identity. In the classic example of the concepts of father and son, the existence of father is dependent upon son. Just as there can be no son without father, there can be no father without son. There can be no understanding of one that does not include and establish reference to the other. The two concepts work together in a reciprocal way to establish mutual identity.

This <u>co</u>-dependency empties concepts and objects of individual existence and works to establish mutual existence. Meditation practice is the effort to come to an intuitive understanding of this co-dependence, and as a result, move from attachment to non-attachment in daily life. The realization that all things are co-dependently arisen works to negate attachment, for it makes no sense to be attached to things that are empty. The reasoning goes: co-dependent arising, therefore emptiness, therefore non-attachment.

For scholars who read Buddhism through co-dependent arising, karma is basically a problem of attachment and can be overcome simply by changing one's perspective. Neither things nor emotions are the problem but the perspective one brings to them. Francis Cook sums up this position well when he states that it is "by means of an absolute oneness with the circumstances themselves, no matter what they are, [that] one paradoxically becomes free from them."[287] It is a "matter of how we see it, a certain perspective."[288] There is an inauthentic self which sees self and things as separate, and an authentic self which results from "restoration of the original unity."[289] Again, I think this is the basic position of any number of scholars who read Buddhist meditation as an act of presencing. Meditation practice then turns experience into pure content without self -- when the self is dropped away there is pure grief, pure joy, pure anger.

The shift from attachment to non-attachment, from inauthentic self to authentic self, is what the co-dependent arising reading sees as enlightenment. This sudden switch to a new form of thinking also marks the authentication of oneself as "one bright pearl." In a sense, then, the self as pearl is very similar to the notion of the self as bright mirror. By clearing away the dust of concepts and opinions in meditation practice, the original clarity of the self as mirror is restored, which allows a bright reflection and pure experience of the world.

This emptiness of thinking and concepts is then extended to people and things: an internal position is extended and becomes an external one. The relationship of objects in the world mirrors the relationship of concepts in thinking. These internal and external perspectives are linked in the image of Indra's Net, a net of infinite proportions with jewels at each of the joins. Each jewel is thus positioned to reflect and be reflected in all the others. When one is able to practice non-attachment, one then authenticates one's original nature and becomes a bright pearl, reflecting and being reflected in all other pearl selves. "One bright Pearl" becomes "Indra's Net."

The second understanding of the meaning of emptiness is as dependent arising, implicit in which is a critique of the limits of the co-dependent arising reading. There is no "co-" or mutuality here. Dependent arising is an emptiness within space and time, both of which are denied in the first reading. Space and time are important, it is argued, because both are necessary for karmic purification and ethical reflection. The dilemma in the co-dependent arising reading can be seen in the father-son example used earlier. The mutuality created in the consistent oscillation between the original points -- father to son, son to father and back -- negates the difference between father and son. Further, it also works to establish one moment in time -- now -- as existing individually without reference to a before or an after. Dependent arising asks: how can "now" have an independent existence apart from the moment before or the moment after?

From the perspective of dependent arising, the equation is not father-son but father-son-daughter-mother-brother-sister-husband-wife, and so on. In other words, there is no return, but a continual movement forward in time and space. For dependent arising, space and time are essential for any Buddhist ethic. The difference in time creates the gap between cause and effect which allows karmic consequence: Moment in time A impacts upon moment in time B. The difference in space creates a separation which allows critical judgement: Person A can evaluate person or situation B. The critique of co-dependent arising from this reading is twofold: presencing in the immediate now negates time and thus the need or opportunity for karmic purification; "all is one" negates space and the possibility of critical evaluation. Dōgen's "bright pearl" here is somewhat problematic, as it seems to suggest some enlightened state beyond time and space. If there were a pearl in the dependent arising reading, it would not be "the self as it is," but an absolute Other, or Buddha.[290]

The ethical critique of the co-dependent arising reading of emptiness is very similar to the ethical critique of Heideggerian thinking (with reference to Heidegger's involvement with Nazism) -- there is no necessary edge within either thinking to block the demonic or prevent a slide into evil actions. Much of what is being written in the area of postmodern ethics seems to be an attempt to come to grips with the implications of this accusation. The on-going investigation into the link between Heideggerian thinking and Nazism highlights the urgency of the query presently being put to Zen studies: given emptiness, whither ethics?

From the perspective of the third reading of emptiness, Buddha essence, both the co-dependent arising and the dependent arising readings of Buddhism fail on the same grounds: neither can account for enlightenment, Dōgen's dropping off of body and mind. The co-dependent arising reading makes enlightenment synonymous with meditation. One is enlightened whenever one meditates. The dependent arising reading (of the Critical Buddhism movement) dismisses the enlightenment of co-dependent arising as completely lacking in ethical ground, and therefore non-Buddhist, but offers no new reading of its own.

The Buddha essence reading accounts for meditation and enlightenment -- Dōgen's cutting the root of thinking and dropping off of body and mind -- by presenting an emptiness which has two aspects. In the same way that light has both a particle and a wave nature, emptiness has both a dependent arising and a Buddha nature. Buddha nature (subtraction/essence) accepts dependent arising (and the need for karmic purification), but denies its ultimacy in decision-making. Buddha essence sees the working of the wave-nature of emptiness as primary in decision-making. While the co-dependent and dependent arising readings approach only the particle nature of emptiness in thinking, the Buddha essence reading (while acknowledging the particle nature of thinking) approaches the wave nature of emptiness through desire and affect. The third reading sees the Buddha nature of emptiness (enlightenment) as an achieved state of desire -- a compassionate nature that is field-sensitive and radiant rather than figure-sensitive and vectored.

The Buddha essence reading sees thinking and desire as inextricably intertwined because all thinking is embodied. The move from father to son to daughter and so on takes place in a pool of affect, emotion and feeling; affect governs what one thinks, how one thinks and the decisions that one makes. Buddhist practice, from the perspective of Buddha essence, is the effort to transform affect from craving into compassion. This third reading posits a ground for an ethics of desire in the distillation of craving into compassion. The force of this ethic lies in the effect compassion has on thinking and decision-making.

To reiterate, this understanding of emptiness as compassion can be explored using the Japanese term for love or desire - *ai*. The same root term "*ai*" can be taken in two completely different directions: one is defiled -- lust and craving; the other is undefiled -- selfless compassion. These two forms of desire can be seen in the two words *aiketsu* and *aigo*, the former referring to the bondage of craving, and the latter to compassionate words. Craving and compassion are thus linked as two natures of desire.

The nature of the relationship between craving and compassion is crucial for the third reading of emptiness, but it is one of difference in degree rather than difference in kind. Again, neither is an Other -- they are not two, but not one either. Figuratively speaking, craving is the wine that becomes brandy of compassion. The wine is not negated or rejected but is transformed. It is not that the wine was bad and the brandy is good, for if one throws the wine away the brandy cannot be made.

How then to turn wine into brandy, craving into compassion? The Buddhist answer is "by burning off karmic defilements." One of the lesser-used Sanskrit terms understood as "defilement," *āsrava* literally means "having outflows" or "having leaks." Following from this, one way to read Buddhist practice (and the two kinds of *ai* or desire) is that it encourages a move from the realm of outflows to the realm without outflows, and that this is best done by the maintaining a practice of no outflowing. To put it another way, one lets go of states of mind which leak or stream.

The move from the outflowing to the non-outflowing realms has been previously explained using the term "subtraction" -- one subtracts defilements in order to reveal essence. Yet the term subtraction is not fully adequate here, and needs to be reconsidered. The use of subtraction is consistent with negative descriptions of Buddhism as goal-less, self-less, and purpose-less, but these are all nods to the perceptual framework of the first aspect of practice, cutting the root of thinking. In other words, while much of the content of the framework is negated, the framework itself remains and is even affirmed. Nothing is posited to take its place. To return to the particle/wave analogy, subtraction is adequate only from the perspective of the particle. From the perspective of the wave, "distillation" better describes Buddhist practice. The work of essence is understood and experienced differently from the perspective of the second aspect of practice, dropping off body and mind. The wine is not subtracted but distilled.

Anger is a good example of a defilement which is distilled. In the Buddha essence reading of emptiness (as opposed to co-dependent arising), anger is a mistake: it is a leak or outflow. Through the practice of meditation, a gap opens up between stimulus and response and it becomes possible to act in ways other than the response that presents itself. In other words, because anger is arising does not mean one need <u>be</u> angry or presence anger.

Anger is a streaming out which prevents the transformation of desire and the construction of the non-leaking realm. It is through burning away tendencies to leak by choosing to act in a non-outflowing manner that the non-leaking realm is constructed. Presencing anger, as one must do if co-dependent arising is primary, is simply not adequate. Buddhist practice transforms the nature of desire by distilling (leaking) anger into (non-leaking or radiant) compassion.

The third reading of emptiness as essence approaches thinking through affect. Changing the nature of bodily force or desire from craving to compassion results in changing the nature of the decisions one makes in daily life. The decisions are made against a different edge: the intention to construct or maintain the radiant luminosity of the non-leaking realm which surrounds, or, actually is, the self.[291]

Returning to the wave/particle analogy, the wave logic or wave sense of compassion is the ultimate truth of emptiness and not the particle logic of co-dependent or dependent arising. Indra's Net is then understood as not only a net of interconnected particle-selves, but also as a wave of brilliant light which exerts a force upon the particles. During the first step of Buddhist practice (before the perspectival shift), the net is seen only as a net: there is no wave, only the interdependence of the particle-selves. However, the wave is always washing through the interdependent particles (like wind or light) and has certain characteristics which impact on the particles. The force of the wave can only be experienced through the existence of the particle-self. Any perception of the nature of the wave is thus dependent upon the state of the particle-self (necessitating the distillation of defiled desire before essence can be realized). Buddhist practice is then the process of cultivating an increased sensitivity to the movement or characteristics of the wave (Buddha essence).[292] The shift from the first aspect of practice to the second is the shift from identification with the particle to identification with the wave: a sudden realization that the "true self" is not a particle at all, but a wave of light. That which governs action is now the force of the wave/light rather than the form and force of the individual particles. Forms are no longer primary.

In other words, dropping off body and mind is the sudden shift in what is primary in orienting perception and guiding decision-making, from particle logic to wave sense -- essence. The sudden shift is made possible by two related practices: first, by gradually changing the nature of one's affective mode by burning off karmic defilements (choosing desire over pleasure); and second, by cultivating a new set of field sensitivities to replace the old figure-vectored sensitivities. The compassionate qualities of the non-vectored state of mind are then able to manifest themselves. For this third reading of emptiness, the realm which radiates compassion is intense and luminous: this is, finally, Dōgen's universe as one bright pearl.

*   *   *   *   *

From the standpoint of the Buddha essence reading, the question "Given emptiness, whither ethics?" calls for an analysis of the grain of nothing, the play of forces at work that precedes and gives birth to thought and action.[293] The play of forces -- the grain of nothing -- can be worked. It can be presenced, "altared" or distilled. And if the play of forces is distilled, then subsequent thinking and action might well change.

But living any philosophy of emptiness (Buddhist or otherwise) is preceded by a theological choice among the different emptinesses available. In the end (or rather, in the beginning), this original choice cannot be grounded by reason but is a matter of faith. Taylor observes, "the judging subject chooses the law with which he or she chooses. The choice of the law of choice is not itself lawful; it is before the law . . . there are no rules to follow in deciding which rules to follow."[294] Nonetheless, deciding which rules to follow is part of questioning one's engagement with the world -- questioning the nature of the gap, threshold, filter, sieve which permits the eye to see. Making a choice among emptinesses is never a neutral decision for it governs the nature of one's engagement with the world.

My purpose here has been to argue that, at this primary level of choice, there are not only two possibilities, presence and difference, but a third -- essence. From the perspective of essence, the debate between presence and difference in postmodern thought, and between co-dependent arising and dependent arising in Buddhism is a disagreement over the nature and function of emptiness in thinking, a disagreement which fails to engage what is primary -- the nature and function of emptiness in desire and affect.

ENDNOTES

[1]Michael E. Zimmerman, 'The Limitations of Heidegger's Ontological Aestheticism," *The Southern Journal of Philosophy* (1989) Vol. XXVIII, Supplement, 187.

[2]Taylor, "Orthodox-y Mending," *Thought* 61/240 (March 1986): 167.

[3]Edith Wyschogrod, *Saints and Postmodernism: Revisioning Moral Philosophy* (Chicago: University of Chicago Press, 1990), 223.

[4]Edith Wyschogrod is extremely critical of this sort of reading of emptiness (as a form of positive desire) and claims it cannot possibly support any kind of ethic. ("Ecstatic experience . . . undoes repression but offers no starting point for action," 214. See also pp. xxiv, 229.) For a similar distinction between difference and positive desire, and a similar critique of the latter, see the chapter on Deleuze (pp. 42-68) in John D. Caputo, *Against Ethics: Contributions to a Poetics of Obligation with Constant Reference to Deconstruction* (Indianapolis: Indiana University Press, 1993). While I agree with the sharp distinction these scholars make between difference and positive desire, I disagree with them on the implications for ethics (as will become fully apparent in chapter five.)

[5]See Nagao's "What remains in *Śūnyatā*," *Mādhyamika and Yogācāra: A Study of Mahāyāna Philosophies* (Albany: State University of New York Press, 1991), 59. Nagao feels strongly that the term "emptiness" has a completely different (and wrongly used), meaning and logic in the *Ratnagotra*.

[6](Atlanta, Georgia: Scholars Press, 1990).

[7]Dōgen deals most directly with meditation in the *Fukanzazengi*, the "Zazengi," and "Zazenshin" fascicles of his *Shōbōgenzō*, and *Bendōhō*. For a concise summary of Dōgen's views on meditation see Hee-Jin Kim's *Dōgen Kigen: Mystical Realist* (Tucson: University of Arizona Press, revised edition, 1987), 55-64. The *Fukanzazengi* -- Rules for Meditation -- is recited daily in Sōtō Zen monasteries.

[8]Martin Heidegger, *What is Called Thinking?* (New York: Harper and Row, 1968), 76. I am also indebted to Jacques Derrida's discussion of this "unthought" in *Typography: Mimesis, Philosophy, Politics* (Cambridge Mass.: Harvard University Press, 1989). See especially pages 11, 14, 20.

[9]Mark C. Taylor, *Altarity* (Chicago: University of Chicago Press, 1987), 111. For an excellent article on clinamen see Warren F. Motte Jr., "Clinamen Redux," *Comparative Literature Studies* 23 (1986): 263-281.

[10]Bloom, *Poetry and Repression: Revisionism from Blake to Stevens* (New Haven: Yale University Press, 1976), 16.

[11]Samuel Taylor Coleridge, *Aids to Reflection*, edited by Henry Nelson Coleridge (Burlington Vermont: Chauncey Goodrich, 1840), 194. Or see instead the volume edited by Thomas Fenby (Liverpool: Edward Howell, 1877), 168-169. (The wording is identical.)

[12]*Webster's Unabridged Dictionary.*

[13]Bernard Faure addresses this "theory gap" in his recent *Chan Insights and Oversights: An Epistemological Critique of the Chan Tradition* (Princeton: Princeton University Press, 1993). He argues (convincingly to me) that Chan texts (especially) function on many different levels--ideological, dialogical, hermeneutical, performative-- and that new and different theoretical approaches are necessary to address these many levels. See especially his introduction (3-11) and chapters three and four ("Rethinking Chan Historiography" and "Alternatives," 89-151).

[14]For instance, Francis Cook and Christopher Ives understand Nāgārjuna to mean that co-dependent arising is synonymous with emptiness whereas Paul Williams reads the same line in Nāgārjuna's *Mūlamadhyamakakārikā* (24:18) totally differently. I will develop this point further in chapter four.

[15]See Kuhn in *The Essential Tension* (Chicago: University of Chicago Press, 1977), xii.

[16]Bernard Faure, *Chan Insights and Oversights*, 274.

[17]Richard Kearney, *The Wake of Imagination* (Minneapolis: University of Minnesota Press, 1988), 280.

[18]Kearney, *Wake of Imagination*, 369.

[19]Victor Farias, *Heidegger and Nazism* (Philadelphia: Temple University Press, 1989), 8.

[20]William J. Richardson, "Heidegger, Truth and Politics," in *Ethics and Danger*, ed. by Arleen B. Dallery and Charles E. Scott (Albany: State University of New York Press, 1992), 18.

[21]Martin Heidegger, *Beitrage Zur Philosophie (Vom Ereignis)*,(Frankfurt Am Main: Vittorio Klostermann, 1989), 380-81, as translated and cited in Joan Stambaugh, *The Finitude of Being* (Albany: State University of New York Press, 1992), 61 (and again, in a slightly different translation, 117).

[22]Martin Heidegger, *On Time and Being*, trans. Joan Stambaugh (New York: Harper and Row, 1972), 68.

[23]Stambaugh, 120.

[24]"Nihilation is neither an annihilation (*Vernichtung*) of what-is, nor does it spring from negation (*Verneinung*). Nihilation cannot be reckoned in terms of annihilation or negation at all. Nothing 'nihilates' (*nichtet*) of itself." "What is Metaphysics," *Existence and Being*, trans. R.F.C. Hull and Alan Crick (Chicago: Henry Regnery Company, 1965), 338-339.

[25]*Discourse on Thinking*, trans. John M. Anderson and E. Hans Freund (New York: Harper and Row, 1966), 82-83.

[26]*Zen Action, Zen Person* (Honolulu: University of Hawaii Press, 1981), 48.

[27]*Discourse*, 61.

[28]*Discourse*, 46.

[29]*Discourse*, 46.

[30]*Discourse*, 47.

[31]*Discourse*, 65.

[32]*Discourse*, 66. A translator's note at the bottom of page 66 in *Discourse on Thinking* indicates that the English move from region to that-which-regions is meant to capture the essence of Heidegger's move from "*Gegend*" to an old variant of "*Gegend*": "*die Gegnet*." The sense of "that-which-regions" is further emphasized by Heidegger's use of the verb "*gegnen*" - "to region."

[33]*Discourse*, 72.

[34]*Discourse*, 83

[35]Heidegger, *On the Way to Language*, trans. Peter D. Hertz (New York: Harper and Row, 1971), 72. For Heidegger on questioning see also pp. 71, 75-76.

[36]I am indebted to Vincent Vycinas's work for stimulating my thinking in this area. See his *Earth and Gods: An introduction to the Philosophy of Martin Heidegger* (The Hague: Martinus Nijhoff, 1969), 82.

[37]See Heidegger's discussion of "lighting and opening" at end of "The End of Philosophy and the Task of Thinking," (trans. Joan Stambaugh) in *Basic Writings* (New York: Harper and Row, 1977), 384-389.

[38]*On the Way to Language*, 32.

[39]*On the Way to Language*, 51-52.

[40]*On the Way to Language*, 52.

[41]*Existence and Being*, 389.

[42]"What is Metaphysics?" 330.

[43]Geoff Bennington and Ian McLeod's translation of *The Truth of Painting*, by Jacques Derrida (Chicago: University of Chicago Press, 1987). See their translator's note p. 120.

[44]*Poetry, Language, Thought*, trans. Albert Hofstadter (New York: Harper and Row, 1971) 33.

[45]Heidegger in the Addendum to "The Origin of the Work of Art," in *Poetry, Language, Thought*, 83.

[46]Of course, not all read (see) Van Gogh's painting in the same way. See Jacques Derrida's reading of Heidegger and the "shoes" in *The Truth in Painting*, 257-382. Among the points Derrida discusses: first, to what degree is Heidegger's argument undermined if these are not peasant shoes at all, but city shoes (the art historian Meyer Shapiro -- Detective Columbo to Derrida -- makes this claim. Following from this, it is interesting to speculate on whether there is a city/country parallel to Heidegger's calculative/meditative split); second, Heidegger's search for an "essence of truth" is inevitably undermined by the abyss (that Heidegger himself points out) in thinking. The metaphor of thinking as a "way" or "road" needs to be juxtaposed with the metaphor of thinking as an "abyss." On this latter point see Robert Denoon Cumming, "The

Odd Couple: Heidegger and Derrida," *Review of Metaphysics* 34 (March 1981): 487-521, and G. Olivier, "Derrida, art and truth," *Journal of Literary Studies* 3 (1985): 27-38.

[47]*Poetry, Language, Thought*, 169.

[48]See Paul Shih-yi Hsiao's article "Heidegger and Our Translation of the *Tao Te Ching*," in *Heidegger and Asian Thought*, edited Graham Parkes (Honolulu: University of Hawaii Press, 1987), 93-101. Heidegger was so demanding in exploring every nuance of meaning in the Chinese characters that only eight of the eighty-one chapters were translated. Exactly which eight chapters these were is not stated in the article.

[49]Ellen M. Chen, *The Tao Te Ching: A New Translation with Commentary* (New York: Paragon House, 1989), 82.

[50]The other major aspect of Tao as function, its supple and soft qualities, is not discussed in chapter 11 but is taken up in other chapters. See especially the water metaphor in chapter 78.

[51]Martin Heidegger, *The Question of Being*, trans. William Kluback and Jean T. Wilde (New York: Twayne Publishers, 1958), 97.

[52]Heidegger, *Philosophy Today* 20 (1976): 289. These stanzas are from Keith Hoeller's translation of one of seven poems or "thoughts" of Heidegger's published in *René Char: Cahiers de l'Herne*, edited by Dominique Fourcade (Editions de l'Herne, Paris, 1971).

[53]For portraits of Vallier see plates 22-30 in *Cézanne: The Late Work*, edited by William Rubin (New York: The Museum of Modern Art, 1977).

[54]Lawrence Gowing, "The Logic of Organized Sensations," *Cézanne: the Late Work*, 70. The paragraph contains references to a number of Cézanne's paintings including one of Vallier. Gowing also notes that Cézanne was working on a profile of Vallier a few days before he died (69).

[55]"A Dialogue on Language," *On the Way to Language*, trans. Peter D. Hertz (New York: Harper and Row, 1971), 1-54. Future references to page numbers in this article are all from this edition.

[56]"Dialogue," 45.

[57]"Dialogue," 46.

[58]"Dialogue," 47.

[59]"Dialogue," 47.

[60]Steven Heine, "The Flower Blossoms `Without Why': Beyond the Heidegger-Kuki Dialogue on Contemplative Language," *Eastern Buddhist* n.s. 23 (Autumn 1990): 75-76.

[61]"Dialogue," 19.

[62]"Dialogue," 41.

[63]"Dialogue," 47.

[64]"Dialogue," 50-51.

[65]"Dialogue," 52.

[66]"What Are Poets For?" *Poetry, Language, Thought*, 89-142.

[67]"The Theological Discussion of `The Problem of a Non-Objectifying Thinking and Speaking in Today's Theology' -- Some Pointers to its Major Aspects," *The Piety of Thinking*, trans. and commentary by James Hart and John Maraldo (Bloomington: Indiana University Press, 1976), 22-31. The letter was originally written on March 11, 1964 as a contribution to the Second Consultation in Hermeneutics held at Drew University in Madison, New Jersey, on April 9-11, 1964. See Heidegger's note in the preface (page 3), and Hopper's discussion of the context for this letter in his introduction to *Interpretation: The Poetry of Meaning*, edited by Stanley Romaine Hopper and David L. Miller (New York: Harcourt, Brace and World, Inc., 1967), xii-xv.

[68]Rilke's fragments are discussed on the last two pages of the "Theological Discussion," 30-31.

[69]Trans. by David Farrell Krell in Basic Writings, 92-112. See also the translation by R.F.C. Hull and Alan Crick in *Existence and Being*, ed. Werner Brock, which includes a postscript Heidegger wrote in 1943. Heidegger wrote an introduction, "The Way Back Into the Ground of Metaphysics" in 1949, which can be found in *Existentialism from Dostoevsky to Sartre*, trans. and ed. by Walter Kaufmann (New York: Meridian Books, 1956), 206-221.

[70]Basic Writings, 102-3.

[71]Martin Heidegger, *Nietzsche Volume IV: Nihilism*, edited, with notes and an analysis, by David Farrell Krell (San Francisco: Harper and Row, 1982).

[72]David Farrell Krell, "Analysis," *Nietzsche volume IV*, 287.

[73]Both are in *Poetry, Language, Thought*.

[74]David Krell, "Analysis," *Nietzsche Volume IV*, 289. As Krell points out, this is not a "crossing out" but a "crossing through."

[75]*Question of Being*, 83.

[76]Heidegger responded to Beaufret's letter of November 10, 1946 one month later, but re-did the letter for publication in 1947. See David Krell's introduction to the "Letter on Humanism" in *Basic Writings*, 190. For Beaufret's question see "Letter on Humanism," trans. Frank A. Capuzzi in collaboration with J. Glenn Gray, *Basic Writings*, 231.

[77]*Basic Writings*, 235.

[78]*Basic Writings*, 240.

[79]*Basic Writings*, 241.

[80]*Basic Writings*, 241.

[81]Reiner Schurmann, Heidegger *On Being and Acting: From Principles to Anarchy* (Bloomington: Indiana University Press, 1990), 287.

[82]*Poetry, Language, Thought*, 44.

[83]Graham Parkes, in the introduction to his edited volume *Heidegger and Asian Thought*, 9-10. Parkes mentions (p. 9) that the story was originally related by Keiji Nishitani in the foreword to one of the volumes of the Japanese edition of the *Collected Works* of D.T. Suzuki.

[84]This comment was related to William Barrett by a "German friend of Heidegger" who found Heidegger reading one of D.T. Suzuki's books when he went to visit. Barrett

includes the story in the introduction he wrote for an edited volume of Suzuki's works. See *Zen Buddhism: Selected Writings of D.T. Suzuki*, edited by William Barrett (Garden City, NY: Doubleday Anchor Books, 1956), xi. The year of the visit and the title of the book are not specified.

[85]See Yasuo Yuasa, "The Encounter of Modern Japanese Philosophy with Heidegger," *Heidegger and Asian Thought*, 155. Yuasa notes that Hajime Tanabe studied with both Husserl and Heidegger in Frieberg in 1922 (157). In addition Shuzo Kuki studied with Husserl and Heidegger before going to Paris to study under Bergson (158). While in Paris Kuki evidently introduced Heidegger's philosophy to the young French student from whom he was learning French -- Jean-Paul Sartre.

[86](Honolulu: University of Hawaii Press, 1990)

[87]Stambaugh, 58.

[88]Stambaugh, 120.

[89]For Kasulis see his (very popular) *Zen Action, Zen Person* (Honolulu: University of Hawaii Press, 1981), especially the section "Heidegger's Gelassenheit: A Western Parallel to [Zen's] No-Mind?" pp. 48-52. See also David Shaner's *The Bodymind Experience in Japanese Buddhism: A Phenomenological Study of Kukai and Dogen* (Albany: State University of New York Press, 1985). Shaner was a student of Kasulis at the University of Hawaii. Shaner's book is basically an explication of the "without thinking" position in Kasulis's *Zen Action, Zen Person*. In addition, see Michael Zimmerman's comparison of Heidegger and Buddhism in the concluding chapter of *Eclipse of the Self: The Development of Heidegger's Concept of Authenticity* (Athens: Ohio University Press, 1981). The connection between Cook, Ives, Abe and Stambaugh will be explored later.

[90]Cook, "Dōgen's View of Authentic Selfhood and its Socio-ethical Implications," Dōgen Studies, edited by William R. LaFleur (Honolulu: University of Hawaii Press, 1985) 136.

[91]Cook, 136-37. The reference to Zimmerman is from *Eclipse of the Self*, 29.

[92]It is theoretically possible for scholars to develop any number of different positions while sharing the common "ground" of the work of emptiness as presence, or presencing.

[93]Michael E. Zimmerman, "The Limitations of Heidegger's Ontological Aestheticism," *The Southern Journal of Philosophy* (1989) Vol. XXVIII, Supplement, 187.

[94]Cook, 142-143.

[95]Kasulis, 50.

[96]Stambaugh, 128.

[97]Cook, 142.

[98]Christopher Ives, *Zen Awakening and Society*, 2. This book, a re-working of Ives' dissertation, fits comfortably into the network of scholarship on different aspects of "Buddhism and presencing." Ives is a long-time student of Masao Abe, to whom the book is dedicated. Abe served as an outside reader of the dissertation and wrote a foreword for the book. Francis Cook was also an outside reader of the dissertation

and met with Ives several times to work on the manuscript. Cook has commented approvingly on Ives understanding of *śūnyatā* in another location: "an excellent presentation of the doctrine of *śūnyatā* as the Mahāyāna Buddhist absolute," in "Reflections on Christopher Ives' Commentary," *Concepts of the Ultimate*, ed. Linda J. Tessier (New York: St. Martin's Press, 1989), 127. Cook is responding to Ives "Emptiness: Soteriology and Ethics in Mahāyāna Buddhism" in Tessier 113-126. Joan Stambaugh (mentioned earlier) dedicated *Impermanence is Buddha-nature* to Masao Abe (and Noriko Kameda). An approving review from Abe appears on the dust-jacket of Stambaugh's book.

[99]Francis Cook, Hua-yen Buddhism: *The Jewel Net of Indra* (University Park: The Pennsylvania State University Press, 1977), 2.

[100]Shohei Ichimura, "An Approach to Dōgen's Dialectical Thinking and Method of Instantiation," *Journal of the International Association of Buddhist Studies* 9/2 (1986): 66.

[101]Ichimura, 73.

[102]Ichimura, 73.

[103]Ichimura, 73.

[104]Cook, "Just this: Buddhist Ultimate Reality," *Buddhist-Christian Studies* 9 (1989): 129. For a similar reading of the Mahāyāna Buddhist tradition (including Dōgen) through Nāgārjuna's *Mūlamadhyamakakārikā* (MMK) and "co-dependent arising" see Christopher Ives, "Emptiness: Soteriology and Ethics in Mahāyāna Buddhism," *Concepts of the Ultimate*, 113-126. (See also Cook's affirmative response to Ives paper on pp. 127-133). Ives acknowledges the help of Masao Abe with the paper. For one example of a reading of Dōgen opposed to Cook see Bernard Faure, *Chan Insights and Oversights*. In Faure's view Cook "reduces Dōgen's teaching to a rather insipid variant of humanism and sees in him a precursor to Nishida's *A Study of Good*" (Faure 265, note 24). (Faure makes specific reference to Cook's "Dōgen's View of Authentic Selfhood and its Socio-ethical Implications," *Dōgen Studies*, 131-149.)

[105]See, for instance, Daizen Victoria, "Japanese Corporate Zen," *Bulletin of Concerned Asian Scholars* 12 (1980): 61-68. I am indebted to Christopher Ives for this reference. See his own discussion of this issue in *Zen Awakening and Society* (Honolulu: University of Hawaii Press, 1992), 51-68. See also Robert H. Sharf "The Zen of Japanese Nationalism," *History of Religions* 33/1 (1993): 1-43.

[106]Paul L. Swanson, "'Zen is not Buddhism': Recent Japanese Critiques of Buddha Nature," *Numen* 40/2 (1993): 115-149. See also Steven Heine, "'Critical Buddhism' (*Hihan Bukkyō*) and the Debate Concerning the 75-fascicle and 12-fascicle *Shōbōgenzō* Texts," *Japanese Journal of Religious Studies* 1994 21/1:37-72.

[107]The reference is to the quotation from William Richardson,"Heidegger, Truth and Politics," in *Ethics and Danger*, 18.

[108]Mark C. Taylor, *Tears* (Albany: State University of New York Press, 1990), 203-4.

[109]Taylor, "On Deconstruction Theology: A symposium on *Erring: A Postmodern A/Theology*," *Journal of the American Academy of Religion* LIV/3 (1986): 553.

[110]*Tears*, 123-144.

[111]This is not to say that Heidegger cannot be read in such a way that his position is much closer to that of Mark Taylor (i.e. a "Heidegger of difference"). Indeed, Mark Taylor does just such a reading of Heidegger. My point is rather that there is strong support for a Heidegger/Gadamer position to which Taylor is opposed.

[112]*Tears*, 134.

[113]*Tears*, 134.

[114]*Tears*, 138.

[115]*Tears*, 141.

[116]Taylor himself explores different meanings of the term in Robert Scharlemann's *Negation and Theology*, 127-128.

[117]*Deconstructing Theology* (New York: Crossroad Publishing and Scholars Press, 1982), 107-129.

[118]*Deconstructing Theology*, 112.

[119]Taylor's spacing of this section is such that the letters and the gap between letters are both equal. See *Deconstructing Theology*, 112-113.

[120]I think the two texts can be seen as products of a similar stage in thinking (and drawing).

[121]*Altarity* (Chicago: University of Chicago Press, 1987), 48.

[122]Taylor, *Tears*, 111.

[123]Mark C. Taylor, *Disfiguring* (Chicago: University of Chicago Press, 1992), 10.

[124]The phrase "total presence" appears frequently in Altizer's work, and is also the title of one of his books. See *Total Presence: The Language of Jesus and the Language of Today* (New York: Seabury Press, 1980).

[125]Let me acknowledge here that my reading of Altizer is limited by my inability to reconcile the "here and now" of point two with the "historical movement to an apocalyptic moment" of point three. If pressed, I could make an attempt at a Buddhist reconciliation through Dōgen's "practice and enlightenment are one and the same" (see the next chapter) but such a reading would deny the sense of "historicity" that is so central to Altizer's work.

[126]Taylor has written two articles on Altizer. See "p. s. fin again," in *Tears*, 55-72, and "Altizer's Originality," *Journal of the American Academy of Religion* 52/3, 570-84.

[127]*Tears*, 76

[128]*Tears*, 76.

[129]*Tears*, 77.

[130]*Negation and Theology*, 128.

[131]"Nothing ending Nothing," *Theology at the End of the Century*, ed. Robert P. Scharlemann (Charlottesville: University of Virginia Press, 1990), 48.

[132]*Theology at the End*, 44.

[133]*Theology at the End*, 47.

[134]"Nothing ending Nothing," 49.

[135]An obvious question is whether or not Mark Taylor's use of "difference" (and "nothing") can be equated with Derrida's use of *différance*. I have only an uncomfortable and provisional answer: not always. While Derrida's *différance* clearly seems to be a process (of temporal deferring and spatial differing), Taylor's "difference" seems to contain some of the noun/verb tension noted in Heidegger's use of "presence" (as described in the previous chapter).

[136]Jacques Derrida, from the transcribed discussion of Asada Akira, Derrida and Karatani Kōjin, "*Choshohi shakai to chishikijin no yakuwari,*" ("The Ultra-Consumer Society and the Role of the Intellectual"), *Asahi jaanaru* (*Asahi Journal*) (May 25, 1984):8-9. This translation and the reference is taken from Marilyn Ivy, "Critical Texts, Mass Artifacts: The Consumption of Knowledge in Postmodern Japan," *The South Atlantic Quarterly* 87:3 (Summer 1988), 439.

[137]Taylor, *Nots*, 3.

[138]*Religion and Nothingness* (Berkeley: University of California Press, 1983), 188-189. It is important to note that most of the essays that make up the book had been published in 1954-55. Nishitani's work (in *Religion and Nothingness*) must be seen as part of a different era of scholarship, more contemporaneous with Heidegger and Tillich than Derrida and Taylor.

[139]Nishitani, 200.

[140]"Emptiness and God," *The Religious Philosophy of Nishitani Keiji*, ed. Taitetsu Unno (Berkeley: Asian Humanities Press, 1989), 70-81. "Buddhist Emptiness and the Crucifixion of God," *The Emptying God: A Buddhist-Jewish-Christian Conversation*, ed. John B. Cobb, Jr., and Christopher Ives (Maryknoll, NY: Orbis Books, 1990), 69-78.

[141]"Nothing Ventured Nothing Gained Nothing Ventured," *Nots* (Chicago: University of Chicago Press, 1993), 56-94.

[142]"Nothing Ventured," 69. These are only a few of the categories Taylor mentions.

[143]"Nothing Ventured," 70.

[144](Chicago: University of Chicago Press, 1984), 118 note 64.

[145]Taylor, "On Deconstruction Theology: A symposium on *Erring: A Postmodern A/Theology,*" *Journal of the American Academy of Religion* LIV/3 (1986): 553.

[146]Frederick Streng's *Emptiness: A Study in Religious Meaning* (New York: Abingdon Press, 1967) has been very helpful to me in writing this section. This translation of the *Mūlamadhyamakakārikā* (MMK: Fundamentals of the Middle Way) is from Streng p. 199.

[147]The translation is from Gadjin Nagao's *The Foundational Standpoint of Mādhyamika Philosophy* translated by John P. Keenan (Albany: State University of New York Press, 1989), 11. The translation in Streng's *Emptiness* reads: "The `originating dependently' we call `emptiness'; This apprehension, i.e., taking into account [all other things], is the understanding of the middle way" (213).

[148]David J. Kalupahana, *Nāgārjuna: The Philosophy of the Middle Way* [with a translation of the *Mūlamadhyamakakārikā*] (Albany: State University of New York Press, 1986), 222-223.

[149]See Streng, 165-166.

[150]*Averting the Arguments (Vigrahāvyavartanī)* 49, in Streng, 226.

[151]Bimal Krishna Matilal, "Is *Prasanga* a Form of Deconstruction?" *Journal of Indian Philosophy* 20 (1992): 356.

[152]Not all scholars read prasanga thought the same way. C.W. Huntington Jr.'s *The Emptiness of Emptiness: An Introduction to Early Indian Mādhyamika* (Honolulu: University of Hawaii Press, 1989) seems to present a reading of prasanga similar to Matilal. Paul Williams, however, vigorously disagrees with Huntington's reading. See Williams' review article "On the Interpretation of Mādhyamika Thought," *Journal of Indian Philosophy* 19 (1991): 191-218.

[153]Matilal, 358-359.

[154]Matilal, 356.

[155]See mainly the panel discussion "On Deconstruction Theology: A Symposium on *Erring*," 523-557.

[156]It is possible to read *différance* in an affirmative way, but this is unacceptable to those who understand its true meaning to be endless negation and deferral. See Mark C. Taylor's "Orthodox-y Mending," *Thought* 61/240 (March 1986):162-171, a review of Robert Magliola's *Derrida on the Mend*. Taylor is highly critical of Magliola's reading of Derrida's *différance* and states: "The reader is forced to conclude that Magliola has not learned the lessons of Derridean deconstruction but remains committed to a form of orthodoxy the time of which has long since passed" (162). And later, "The confusion of differential relation and mutuality is closely bound to the most devastating misunderstanding that haunts this confused book. Contrary to every expectation, Magliola attempts to enlist Derrida's understanding of *différance* in a defense of divine unity" (170).

[157]Taylor, "Orthodoxy," 167.

[158]Taylor, "Orthodoxy," 169.

[159]It would be interesting to know if the work of Derrida and/or Taylor has played any part in the development of this movement.

[160]"nO nOt nO," *Derrida and Negative Theology*, edited Harold Coward and Toby Forshay (Albany: State University of New York Press, 1992), 176. All references to this article are to the version in this publication.

[161]"nO nOt nO," 176.

[162]"nO nOt nO," 177. Earlier in the article Taylor endnotes Freud's comment on negation: "To negate something in a judgment is, at bottom, to say: This is something which I should prefer to repress. . . . With the help of the symbol of negation, thinking frees itself from the restrictions of repression and enriches itself with material that is indispensable for its proper functioning" (197 -- from *The Standard Edition of the Complete Psychological Works of Sigmund Freud*, vol. 19, trans. James Strachey (London: Hogarth Press, 1961), 236.

[163]See again the discussion of Heidegger's use of these three dots in the previous chapter.

[164]Jacques Lacan, *Four Fundamental Concepts in Psychoanalysis*, 63-64 as quoted by Taylor in *Altarity*, 110. Taylor has included the original French text in the square brackets.

[165]Taylor quoting from *Lacan's Four Fundamental Concepts (FFC)* in *Altarity*, 110.

[166]*Altarity*, 232.

[167]Taylor quoting from Blanchot in *Altarity*, 234. *PA* is Blanchot's *Le Pas au-dela* (Paris: Gallimard, 1973). *EI* is Blanchot's *L'Entretien infini* (Paris: Gallimard, 1969). Translations by Taylor.

[168]*Altarity*, 237.

[169]*Altarity*, 237.

[170]"nO nOt nO," 190.

[171]"nO nOt nO," 171.

[172]"nO nOt nO," 190.

[173]"nO nOt nO," 190.

[174]Taylor quoting from Heidegger's *Poetry, Language, Thought* (PLT) in *Altarity*, 84.

[175]"nO nOt nO," 172.

[176]I am indebted to an article by James DiCenso for stimulating this line of thinking. See his article "Deconstruction and the Philosophy of Religion: World Affirmation and critique," *Philosophy of Religion* 31 (1992): 29-43.

[177]"nO nOt nO," 190.

[178]Heidegger, *Poetry, Language, Thought*, 63 as quoted in Taylor's *Altarity*, 50.

[179]Caputo acknowledges that the tennis game suggestion comes originally from Diane Michelfelder. Caputo adds what he calls a "Levinasian twist" to Michelfelder's example by adding the "higher and lower" to the self/other "play." See his article "Beyond Aestheticism: Derrida's Responsible Anarchy," *Research in Phenomenology* 18 (1988): 68-69. Michelfelder's remarks were made at a 1987 symposium on Gadamer and Derrida. See also her article "Derrida and the Ethics of the Ear," *The Question of the Other*, ed. Arleen B. Dallery and Charles E. Scott (Albany: State University of New York Press, 1989), 47-54.

[180]*Tears*, 143.

[181]*Erring*, 146.

[182]*Erring*, 147.

[183] *Erring*, 147.

[184]Takasaki's translation of the *Ratnagotravibhāga*, p. 300. See Jikido Takasaki, *A study on the Ratnagotravibhāga Being a Treatise on Tathāgatagarbha Theory of Mahāyāna Buddhism* (Rome: Is. M.E.O. Serie Orientale Roma BD XXXIII, 1966).

[185]Brian Edward Brown, *The Buddha Nature: A Study of the Tathāgatagarbha and the Ālayavijñāna* (Delhi: Motilal Banarsidass, 1991), 79-80.

[186]This oft-quoted line is from the fascicle "Busshō" (Buddha-nature). Dōgen begins the fascicle as follows: "Sakyamuni Buddha said, 'All sentient beings without exception have the Buddha-nature. Tathagata abides forever without change'" (from the *Nirvana*

sutra, chapter 27). See the translation by Norman Waddell and Abe Masao "*Shōbōgenzō* Buddha-nature, Part I," *Eastern Buddhist* n.s. 8/2 (1975): 96-97.

[187]Robert M. Gimello, review of *The Buddha Within: Tathāgatagarbha Doctrine According to the Shentong Interpretation of the Ratnagotravibhāga* by S.K. Hookham, The Journal of Asian Studies 51/3 (August 1992): 624.

[188]This is especially true if one understands Nāgārjuna to be the author of a "hymnic corpus" in addition to his "scholastic corpus" (the MMK being a part of the latter). For a discussion of this point see David Seyfort Ruegg, *The Literature of the Mādhyamika School of Philosophy in India* (Weisbaden: Otto Harrassowitz, 1981), 31-32. Ruegg points out that parts of the "hymnic corpus" seem close to Tathāgatagarbha theory. This, then, would be a third reading of Nāgārjuna. For an example of a reading of Nāgārjuna which emphasizes this more "religious" aspect, see K. Venkata Ramanan, *Nāgārjuna's Philosophy as Presented in the Mahā-Prajñāpāramitā-Sastra* (Rutland Vermont: Charles E. Tuttle Co. 1966; reprint ed. Delhi: Motilal Banarsidass, 1975). This aspect is especially apparent in Ramanan's discussion of the "unborn" and "unconditioned." (See, for instance, pp. 261-263, - the catch here is that there is some debate over the authorship of the *Mahā-prajñāpāramitā-Sastra*). For a discussion of different readings of Mādhyamika (including opposed readings of the same textual references in Nāgārjuna's MMK) see Paul William's review essay "On the interpretation of Mādhyamika thought," *Journal of Indian Philosophy* 19 (1991): 191-218. Williams is reviewing C.W.Huntington Jr.'s *The Emptiness of Emptiness: An Introduction to early Indian Mādhyamika.*

[189]Nagao, *Mādhyamika and Yogācāra*, 59.

[190]See S.K. Hookam's discussion of the term "Tathāgatagarbha" in *The Buddha Within: Tathāgatagarbha Doctrine According to the Shentong Interpretation of the Ratnagotravibhāga* (Albany: State University of New York Press, 1991), 99-100.

[191]The move to Tathagatagarbha thought does not, of course, escape the issue of multiple readings. It is quite possible to do a "Mādhyamika" reading of Tathāgatagarbha literature. Indeed, a section of Minoru Kiyota's paper on Tathāgatagarbha (referenced earlier) is titled "A Mādhyamika interpretation of Tathāgatagarbha" (see p. 217). The interpretive split over the meaning of emptiness in the scholarly tradition extends to readings of exactly the same texts. Further, it may well be that this split in the scholarly tradition mirrors a split in the Buddhist tradition itself. For instance there is a split in the Tibetan Buddhist tradition between the "emptiness of self" school (Rangtong) and the "emptiness of other" school (Shentong - that Ultimate Reality is empty of what is other than itself -- from Dolpopa of the Jonangpa school of 14th century Tibet). S.K. Hookham (in *The Buddha Within*), notes how complex the issue can be when she states that "some teachers choose to expound a certain scripture from a Rantong point of view for some pupils and the same scripture from the Shentong point for others. . . " (14). For a different perspective on the Jonangpa school see David Seyfort Ruegg, "On the Dge Lugs Pa Theory of the Tathāgatagarbha," *Pratidanam*, edited by J.C. Heesterman et. al., (The Hague: Mouton, 1968), 500-509. Ruegg introduces an additional complication when he suggests that the same doctrine (in this article, the

Tathāgatagarbha) may be seen to have "explicit and certain meaning" (*nes don = nītārtha*)" by one group and of "intentional and indirect meaning (*dran don = neyārtha*)" by another (501).

[192]Gadjin Nagao states: "The theory that the Tathāgatagarbha is empty as well as non-empty is established on the authority of the *Śrīmālādevī*; but here the items negated are contaminations only, while the Tathāgatagarbha is never negated. . . . In this case, the subject of 'is not' (negation) and 'is' (affirmation) are different from each other, the former being defilement and the latter virtue. In the Madhyānta, however, one and the same entity (*abhūtaparikalpa*) is the subject of both 'is not' and 'is,' of both existence and non-existence. The duality of subject and object, which is essential to *abhutaparikalpa*, is negated; hence *śūnyatā* is. And that very emptiness of what is empty is never negated, is never nonexistent. . . .hence, 'existence of non-existence.'... But such a double structure is not conceivable in the case of the Tathāgatagarbha." See Nagao's *Mādhyamika and Yogācāra*, 57-58.

[193]Paul Williams has been very helpful to me here. See especially his (already cited) review article on Huntington's *Emptiness of Emptiness*, especially pp. 205, 207-208.

[194]Dōgen does not use the term "emptiness" (*kū*) frequently. The two most well known examples are the titles of the fascicles "Kūge" (Flowers of emptiness) and "Kokū" (Universal Emptiness). Dōgen's "ultimate reality" is more often expressed in terms of "buddha nature," "original face," or "true nature," or more poetic renderings such as "one bright pearl." Scholars of Buddhism, however, have come to use the term "emptiness" frequently with reference to Dōgen, and it seems to be almost synonymous with many of Dōgen's more oft-used terms. That is, the discovery of one's "original face" is interpreted to be a realization of "emptiness." Clearly, establishing the nature of the "emptiness" thus realized is crucial to interpreting Dōgen.

[195]Minoru Kiyota sees "concern with karma" as one way to distinguish between Mādhyamika, which "seemed to have dismissed the subject with its doctrine of emptiness" and Yogācāra, which "picked it up again, examined it in the context of alaya consciousness and emphasized meditative discipline to transform that human consciousness." "Tathāgatagarbha Thought: A Basis of Buddhist Devotionalism in East Asian," *Japanese Journal of Religious Studies* 12/2-3 (1985): 224. My point here is that a "sense" or "logic" different from (or in addition to) co-dependent arising may be necessary in order to develop a more comprehensive theory of karma.

[196]Paul Williams sees a logical connection between Tathāgatagarbha thought and Dōgen's Zen Buddhism. In his *Mahāyāna Buddhism: The Doctrinal Foundations* (Routledge: New York, 1989) he includes a section "Dōgen on the Buddha Nature" in his chapter "The *Tathāgatagarbha* (Buddha-essence/Buddha-nature)." See also David Ruegg,"The Jo Nan Pas: A School of Buddhist Ontologists According to the GRUB MTHA SEL GYI ME LON," *Journal of the American Oriental Society* 83 (1963): 73-91. Ruegg suggests there may be some similarities between Jonanpa doctrines, "certain works attributed to Aśvaghosa" and "certain schools of Chinese and Japanese Buddhism, including Ch'an/Zen and T'ien-t'ai/Tendai" (footnote 1b, 73-74).

[197]Alex Wayman and Hideko Wayman, *The Lion's Roar of Queen Śrīmālā* (New York: Columbia University Press, 1974), xi, 1. The dates of the scriptures come from Waymans' introduction as well. The inclusion of the *Laṅkāvatāra sūtra* and the *Awakening of Faith* within the Tathāgatagarbha literatures is somewhat problematic, as both these sutras identify the term "Tathāgatagarbha" with the "store-house consciousness" (alaya-vijñana). This is a crucial point and for some has been a reason for excluding them from the Tathāgata-garbha stream (See Wayman, *Lion's Roar* 44, 52-53). This section will refer to the *Śrīmālā sūtra* and the *Ratnagotravibhāga* as representatives of Tathāgatagarbha thought.

[198]Diana Mary Paul's translation from her *The Buddhist Feminine Ideal: Queen Śrīmālā and the Tathāgatagarbha* (Missoula, Montana: Scholars Press, 1980), 197.

[199]Wayman divides the *Śrīmālā sūtra* into four chapters in his translation. The *Ratnagotravibhāga's* citations all come from what he has designated as the third chapter "Clarifying the final meaning." See *Lion's Roar*, 6.

[200]Takasaki's translation of the *Ratnagotravibhāga* p. 300. See Jikido Takasaki, *A Study on the Ratnagotravibhāga Being a Treatise on Tathāgatagarbha Theory of Mahāyāna Buddhism* (Rome: Is.M.E.O. Serie Orientale Roma BD XXXIII, 1966).

[201]Takasaki, 305.

[202]Takasaki, 308. Brown states: "The fault here is his insistence not only upon the unreality of all defects and defilements, but also of all virtues which are on the contrary, real and pure by nature." See p. 151.

[203]Takasaki, 268-269.

[204]Takasaki, 270-271.

[205]Brown suggests that the two traditions may have developed opposing strategies to counter Abhidharma beliefs. He states: "The Ratnagotra characteristically does not counter this subtle substantiation (i.e., the assumption of the unqualified reality of evanescence, suffering, non-ego, and impurity) by the Mādhyamikan application of the binary *śūnyatā-śūnyatā*. Instead, it proposes an alternate meditational subject. Rather than the continual contemplation of phenomena as *anitya, duhkha, anātma* and *aśubha*, one should concentrate upon and comprehend the Tathāgata-embryo as the supreme eternity (*nitya-pāramitā*), the supreme bliss (*sukha-pāramitā*), the supreme unity (*ātma-pāramitā*) and the supreme purity (*śubha-pāramitā*)" (136-7).

[206]Alex Wayman's translation of the *Ratnagotravibhaga* in *The Lion's Roar of Queen Śrīmālā*, 47.

[207]Dōgen was in China from the first to the third years of the *Pao-ch'ing* era (1225-1227). *Hōkyōki* (Chinese *Pao-ch'ing chi*) is thus "Record of the *Pao-ch'ing* Era." For the textual history of the *Hōkyōki* see Takahashi James Kodera, *Dōgen's Formative Years in China* (Boulder: Prajna Press, 1980), 113-116.

[208]Kodera, 124.

[209]Kodera, 125.

[210]Kodera, 180.

[211]Kodera, 133.

²¹²Kodera, 180, note 43. Kodera goes on to compare this view with a line from Nāgārjuna "If you practice almsgiving, you will eliminate greed; you must practice almsgiving singlemindedly in order to remove the five defilements. The removal of the five defilements is meditation" (*Ta-chih-tu lin* 17). This lends support those who argue that even in Nāgārjuna (co)dependent arising need not be seen as primary. [i.e. (Co)dependent arising could well be the conventional rather than the ultimate truth.]

²¹³N. A. Waddell, "Dōgen's *Hōkyō-ki - part one*," *Eastern Buddhist* n.s. 10/2 (October 1977): 132, note 53. See also the discussion of zazen and the "five restraints" in part two, Eastern Buddhist n.s. 11/1 (May 1978): 73-74.

²¹⁴Yuho Yokoi, *Zen Master Dōgen: An Introduction with Selected Writings* (Tokyo: Weatherhill, 1976), 156. Dōgen is quoting from the *Mo-ho-chih-kuan* here, a work on meditation by the T'ien-t'ai teacher Chih-i.

²¹⁵Yokoi, 158. Again, Dōgen is quoting from the *Mo-ho-chih-kuan*. It is interesting to compare the view of women in this quotation, or the previous quotation ("when he touched the delicate soft skin of a woman, and fell victim to sexual desire, he realized he had not attained the third stage either") with the quite different view of women contained in a Tantric Buddhist text written by a female teacher: "Seeing a delightful woman/ As enlightenment spontaneously appearing in embodied form,/ A Buddha gazes with passion and playfulness, and/ Desire for pleasure and bliss arises" (from Sahajayoginīcintā's *Realization of Reality through its Bodily Expressions* -- Sanskrit *Vyaktabhāvānugata-tattva-siddhi*). Although at first glance these quotations seem to suggest completely opposed positions on desire, it may not be quite that simple. The issue in Dōgen's quotations is not women, but the monk's "immature" response to women: objectified lust or desire. This seems to be at least part of the issue (if not the central issue) in Tantric Buddhist practice as well, where the energy of lust is used and transformed into spiritual bliss (but lust itself cannot remain). See Miranda Shaw's *Passionate Enlightenment: Women in Tantric Buddhism* (Princeton: Princeton University Press, 1994), especially pp. 179-194. The quotation from Sahajayoginicintā comes from Shaw, page 184. I will take this issue up in more detail in the next chapter.

²¹⁶English translations of fascicles of the *Shōbōgenzō* appear in quotation marks (e.g. "One Bright Pearl") while independent works are italicized (e.g. *Guidelines for Studying the Way*).

²¹⁷The translation is from *Moon in a Dewdrop: Writings of Zen Master Dōgen*, edited by Kazuaki Tanahashi (San Francisco: North Point Press, 1985), 42. See also Hee-Jin Kim's similar translation in his *Dōgen Kigen: Mystical Realist*, 261-262.

²¹⁸Yuho Yokoi, "Zazenshin," *The Shōbō-genzō* (Tokyo: Sankibo Buddhist Bookstore, 1986), 139-140. It is important to note that this section of the fascicle is not included in the edited version in Hee-Jin Kim's *Flowers of Emptiness* (Lewiston NY: The Edwin Mellen Press, 1985). I understand Dōgen's use of the "transmission of the Law" here to be the equivalent of (or to occur when) "body and mind drop away." Although Dōgen does not link these in this quotation, the move seems supported by discussion earlier in the fascicle.

[219]From Francis Cook's translation in his *Sounds of the Valley Streams: Enlightenment in Dōgen's Zen* (Albany: State University of New York Press, 1989), 66.

[220]Norman Waddell and Abe Masao translation from *Eastern Buddhist* n.s. vol. 5, no. 2 (1972): 135.

[221]"Keisei Sanshoku" ("Sounds of Valley Streams, Forms of the Mountains"), from Francis Cook's translation in his *How to Raise an Ox* (Los Angeles: Center Publications, 1978), 101.

[222]"Dōtoku" ("Expression"), from Cook, *Sounds*, 102.

[223]Philip B. Yampolsky, *The Platform Sutra of the Sixth Patriarch* (New York: Columbia University Press, 1967), 130-132.

[224]Yampolsky, 131.

[225]Cook, *Sounds*, 72.

[226]Cook, "Just This: Buddhist Ultimate Reality," 139. I have used Cook here, and elsewhere in this chapter, because he offers such a comprehensive theory on Dōgen based on different fascicles of the *Shōbōgenzō*. However, I should point out that a number of scholars refer to "One Bright Pearl" to explain a "presencing" or "co-dependent arising is primary" reading of Buddhist practice. See, for instance, David Shaner, *The Bodymind Experience in Japanese Buddhism*, 169. In addition see David Loy, "Indra's Postmodern Net," *Philosophy East and West* 43/3 (July 1993): 481-510. Loy approaches Indra's Net through difference rather than presence. However, as Loy's difference ends up being an affirmative difference, his reading seems compatible with Cook's position.

[227]*Sounds*, 73.

[228]*Sounds*, 74.

[229]*Sounds*, 75.

[230]Norman Waddell and Masao Abe's translation, in *Eastern Buddhist* new series IV no.2 (1971): 113.

[231]Cook translates: "Because of its priority over its functional manifestations, this principle remains as something ungraspable even in the midst of its functioning" (*Sounds*, 73). Kim translates "Because this is a truth prior to the origin of things, its essence is beyond our control" (*Flowers of Emptiness*, 127).

[232]*Sounds*, 74.

[233]I follow Arun Balasubramaniam here in believing that the parallels between Buddhism and quantum physics are "not parallels of identity but parallels of analogy." See his summary of the use of this analogy and its problematic nature: "Explaining Strange Parallels: The Case of Quantum Mechanics and Mādhyamika Buddhism," *International Philosophical Quarterly* 32/2, Issue 126 (June 1992): 205-223. The wave-particle analogy can be used in many ways to illustrate diverse (and sometimes opposing) understandings of Buddhism.

[234]Reiho Masunaga, *A Primer of Sōtō Zen: A translation of Dōgen's Shōbōgenzō Zuimonki* (Honolulu: University of Hawaii Press, 1975), 21. A similar translation appears in Thomas Cleary's *Record of Things Heard* (Boulder: Prajna Press, 1980), 18-19.

[235] *Japanese-English Buddhist Dictionary* (Tokyo: Daitō Shuppansha, 1965). Steve Heine translates "*gyōji*" as "sustained exertion," and notes "*gyō*" means activity, movement, exertive effort; "*ji*" means to hold, maintain, or sustain unrelentingly." See his *Existential and Ontological Dimensions of Time in Heidegger and Dōgen* (Albany: State University of New York Press, 1985), 176-77, note 45. Hee-Jin Kim translates "*gyōji*" as "activity" but uses it in a way that also suggests effort, exertion and actualization. See Kim's discussion of "*gyōji*" as an aspect of Dōgen's zazen on 64-66 of *Dōgen Kigen Mystical Realist*.

[236] Kim, *Flowers of Emptiness*, 75. Again, I equate "actualizing a buddha" with "dropping off body and mind," the second aspect of practice. Waddell and Abe translate slightly differently: "As for the truth of the Buddha-nature: the Buddha-nature is not incorporated prior to attaining Buddhahood; it is incorporated upon the attainment of Buddhahood. The Buddha-nature is always manifested simultaneously with the attainment of Buddhahood." The Waddell/Abe translation continues: "This truth should be deeply, deeply penetrated in concentrated practice. There has to be twenty or even thirty years of diligent Zen practice." In footnotes, Kim and Abe/Waddell stress the importance of the passage for clarifying the relationship between practice and enlightenment. See Norman Waddell and Abe Masao, "*Shōbōgenzō* Buddha-Nature Part II," *Eastern Buddhist* 9/1 (1976): 88.

[237] "Bendōwa," in Kim, Mystical Realist, 65.

[238] For a related but slightly different view of this process see Shigenori Nagatomo's analysis of "casting off the body and mind" as a "transformation of negative affectivity into positive affectivity" in his "An Analysis of Dōgen's 'Casting off Body and Mind,'" *International Philosophical Quarterly* 27/3, #107 (September 1987): 227-242. In my reading, Nagatomo makes the mistake of collapsing the second aspect of "studying the way" into the first, and thus reducing "dropping off body and mind" to "cutting the root of thinking." From this perspective, Nagatomo's work is very helpful in understanding the affective component of the first aspect of "studying the way" ("cutting the root of thinking"), but is not helpful in accounting for the perspectival shift involved in the second aspect ("dropping off of body and mind"). To put it another way, I see Nagatomo's philosophy of "attunement" as a "gradualism" that is limited in its usefulness by its inability to account for the "sudden" in Dōgen.

[239] "Gyōji," in Heine, 137. Cook translates: "Conditional arising is continuous practice, but continuous practice is not conditionally generated, and this you should diligently seek to understand." Ox, 176.

[240] Again, Shigenori Nagatomo articulates this perspective very well. See his *Attunement Through the Body* (Albany: State University of New York Press, 1992).

[241] *Nietzsche and Philosophy*, trans. Hugh Tomlinson (New York: Columbia University Press, 1983), 4.

[242] The reference is to the use of the quotation from Bernard Faure, *Chan Insights and Oversights*, 274.

[243]"Guidelines for Studying the Way," *Moon in a Dewdrop: Writings of Zen Master Dōgen*, 42. The *Gakudō Yōjinshū* is one of Dōgen's independent works (and not a part of the *Shōbōgenzō*).

[244]*Japanese-English Buddhist Dictionary* (Tokyo: Daitō Shuppansha, 1965), 4. See Steven Heine's discussion of the double meaning of *ai* in Buddhism in his "Multiple Dimensions of Impermanence in Dōgen's "*Genjōkōan*," *Journal of the International Association of Buddhist Studies* 4/2 (1981): 52.

[245]Jikido Takasaki, *An Introduction to Buddhism*, translated by Rolf W. Giebel (Tokyo: The Toho Gakkai, 1987), 119-120, 167.

[246]I draw mainly on the chapter "November 28, 1947: How Do You Make Yourself a Body Without Organs?" in Deleuze and Guattari's *A Thousand Plateaus*, trans. Brian Massumi (Minneapolis: University of Minnesota Press, 1988), 149-166.

[247]The quotation appears in the middle of a reference to Gregory Bateson. Deleuze and Guattari write: "A plateau is always in the middle, not at the beginning or the end. . . . Gregory Bateson uses the word 'plateau' to designate something very special: a continuous, self-vibrating region of intensities whose development avoids any orientation toward a culmination point or external end. Bateson cites Balinese culture as an example: '. . . Some sort of continuing plateau of intensity is substituted for (sexual) climax,' war or a culmination point" (*Thousand Plateaus* 22). The reference is to Bateson's *Steps to an Ecology of Mind* (New York: Ballantine Books, 1972), 113.

[248]I wonder how much of Deleuze's work is dependent on a model or metaphor developed from male sexual experience. This brings up a number of related questions: how would a model developed from female experience be different? Can any differences between male and female sexuality also be extended to the experience of anger and fear? Are "male" and "female" better seen as two ends of a spectrum upon which any one individual (regardless of genitalia) could be placed at any point? Is this point fixed? Does the point drift? If so, how?

[249]Deleuze discusses these and other instances in a variety of places in *Thousand Plateaus*, including 22 (sexual climax, war), 154 (pleasure as discharge), 227 (fear). The Buddhist question here might be whether Deleuze's statements on sexual desire are of "explicit" or "indirect" meaning.

[250]Brian Massumi, *A user's guide to Capitalism and Schizophrenia: Deviations from Deleuze and Guattari* (Cambridge Mass.: Swerve Editions, MIT Press, 1992), 38. I have found Massumi's work very helpful in developing my own reading of Deleuze and am greatly indebted to his book.

[251]Massumi, 43.

[252]"Burning off defilements" may well lead to actual physical changes in the way the brain operates. Recent advances in medical technology make it possible to start doing research in this area. See Sandra Blakesee's article "Behavior Therapy Can Change How the Brain Functions, Researchers Say," in the *New York Times* (September 16, 1992): A20, or the scientific article (upon which the article was partially based) by Lewis R. Baxter Jr., et. al., "Caudate Glucose Metabolic Rate Changes With Both

Drug and Behavior Therapy for Obsessive-Compulsive Disorder," *Archives of General Psychiatry* 49 (September 1992): 681-689.

[253]Pleasure and desire (in my usage) can be partly distinguished by whether or not a form or object is present -- pleasure has an object while desire does not. I look forward to doing future work comparing and contrasting this position (and thus developing it further) with that of different schools of Tantric Buddhism. *In Passionate Enlightenment: Women in Tantric Buddhism*, Miranda Shaw quotes from a Tantric Buddhist text: "Human pleasure, with its identifiable characteristics,/ Is the very thing that,/ When its characteristics are removed,/ Turns into spiritual ecstasy. . ." (Shaw 188, from Sahajayoginicinta's *Realization of Reality through its Bodily Expressions -- Sanskrit Vyaktabhāvānugata-tattva-siddhi*). The question (for me) is, exactly what are the "identifiable characteristics" that distinguish the desire of ordinary pleasure from the desire of spiritual ecstasy, and how does the removal of these characteristics change the nature, quality and experience of desire? Even in Shaw's account of what is clearly a non-celibate practice, states of lust, or "objectified desire" seem to be a problem. As she puts it, "the sexual yoga for transforming passion to divine ecstasy should be performed in a state of meditative awareness that is free from lust, ordinary attachment, and conceptual thought" (169), and the move from a "conditional bliss dependent on the senses" to "spiritual ecstasy" requires going "beyond desires dependent on sense objects" (188 specifically, and 177-194 in general). Further complicating the issue of the difference between the desire of ordinary pleasure and the desire of spiritual ecstasy, Lama Yeshe states that one of the differences between tantric embrace and ordinary sexual contact is that "while in ordinary sex it is the man who enters the woman's body, in true tantric embrace it is the woman's energy that penetrates the man." See his Introduction to Tantra: *A Vision of Totality*. (London: Wisdom Publications, 1987), 148. (One wonders whether Herbert Guenther had this difference in mind when he stated -- on the dust jacket of Shaw's book -- that "*Passionate Enlightenment* is a penetrating investigation into the role of women in the area of Tantric Buddhism . . ."!)

[254]Again, the psychological studies seem to measure more or less dependence on the visual field (with little account of affect). In general, those with field dependent perceptual styles (more dependent on the visual field for processing information) are thought to be at a disadvantage. The possibility that those persons may have an advantage in processing information in ways other than the visual (e.g. affect) does not seem to have been heavily researched.

[255]The temptation here is to set up an opposition between (visual) perception-based differences in kind and affect-based differences in degree. However, it is far more complicated than this, as the two sensitivities seem to lie on lines that intersect. For an interesting account of an attempt to deal with the hunter/farmer problem in field research, see Jan M.H. Van De Koppel, *A Developmental Study of the Biaka Pygmies and the Bangandu* (Lisse: Swets & Zeitlinger, 1983).

[256]This is not to suggest that Monet is an arahat!

[257]The suggestion here is that it may be useful to look at Buddhist practice as sophisticated training in field dependent cognitive processing. It seems possible that such training may involve actual physiological changes within the brain -- a "re-wiring" of the neurological circuits. This line of thinking has been provoked by my reading of articles (none of which mention Buddhism) in *Field Dependence-Independence: Cognitive Styles Across the Life Span* edited by Seymour Wapner and Jack Demick (Hillsdale NJ: Lawrence Erlbaum Associates, 1991). I hope to pursue this line of thought in future research.

[258]*Thousand Plateaus*, 494.

[259]*Thousand Plateaus*, 494.

[260]*Thousand Plateaus*, 492.

[261]Gilles Deleuze, "Michel Tournier and the World without Others," *The Logic of Sense* (New York: Columbia University Press, 1990), 301-320. See also Alphonso Lingis, "Deleuze on a Deserted Island," *Philosophy and Non-Philosophy since Merleau-Ponty* ed. Hugh J. Silverman (New York: Routledge, 1988), 152-173.

[262]Michel Tournier, *Friday*, trans. Norman Denny (New York: Pantheon Books, 1985 [1967]).

[263]Deleuze, *The Logic of Sense*, 307.

[264]Deleuze, *The Logic of Sense*, 309.

[265]Deleuze, *The Logic of Sense*, 315.

[266]Deleuze, *The Logic of Sense*, 308.

[267]Philip B. Yampolsky, *The Platform Sutra of the Sixth Patriarch* (New York: Columbia University Press, 1967), 130-132.

[268]I see this use of Taylor's difference to be equivalent to Derrida's *différance*.

[269]I am guided here by my reading of Rodolpe Gasché's *The Tain of the Mirror: Derrida and the Philosophy of Reflection* (Cambridge, Mass: Harvard University Press, 1986), and Irene E. Harvey's *Derrida and the Economy of Différance* (Bloomington: Indiana University Press, 1986).

[270]Gasché, *Tain of the Mirror*, 219.

[271]Gasché, *Tain of the Mirror*, 221.

[272]Gasché, *Tain of the Mirror*, 225.

[273]This is how I read Dōgen's "total exertion." It is a reading of meditation clearly opposed to that presented in the Buddhist sections of chapters two and three.

[274]See the seminal 1956 paper on double bind theory by Gregory Bateson et.al., "Toward a Theory of Schizophrenia," reprinted in *Beyond the Double Bind: Communication and Family Systems, Theories, and Techniques with Schizophrenics*, edited by Milton B. Berger (New York: Brunner/Mazel, 1978), 5-27.

[275]The fascicle further indicates a lesser stage of arahatship when those emotions still arise, but do so presumably with less intensity in a context where they are known to be symptoms of "false notions of existence" and are therefore not acted upon. However, the monks were "overwhelmed" by these emotions and thus concluded they were not even at the third stage of arahatship.

[276]I thank Ruth Ost and David Miller for their help with this especially nettlesome section.

[277]Rosi Braidotti may be suggesting something similar in her reading of Deleuze when she talks about envisaging "energetic or affective relations as the basis for the production of meaning." See her *Patterns of Dissonance* (New York: Routledge, 1991), 112.

[278]It is not surprising that not all are able to do this consistently. This would be a possible explanation for one of the questions Christopher Ives (among many others) raises about the conduct of Buddhist teachers. This question might be put, If all Roshis are enlightened, how is it that a Roshi can makes mistakes? See his *Zen Awakening and Society*, 111-113. The "answer" would be that, with reference to this one question, enlightenment is less like leaping a hurdle of delusion (which is then forever left behind) and more like riding a bicycle (which one can fall off at any time).

[279]Using the prefix "es" gives a more accurate rendering than the prefix "un": not "un-sense" but "es-sense." Unsense connotes negation while essence connotes distillation, a term developed in chapter six.

[280]Cleary, *Shōbōgenzō: Zen Essays by Dōgen.* (Honolulu: University of Hawaii Press, 1986), 9. Cleary's reference is to the Taishō Shinshū Daizōkyō vol. 47, p. 534a.

[281]Cleary, 19. Cleary's reference is to the *Eihei Kōroku*, scroll 4.

[282]See Kim's translation of the fascicle "Ikka Myōju" (One Luminous Pearl) in *Flowers of Emptiness*, 126-132. The idea of translucence or transparency is important in my reading of dropping off body and mind as a switch from "forms are primary" to "forms are not primary."

[283]I borrow the term from Neal Donner (but, I think, use it differently). See his "Sudden and Gradual Intimately Conjoined: Chih-i's T'ien-t'ai View," *Sudden and Gradual: Approaches to Enlightenment in Chinese Thought*, edited by Peter N. Gregory (Honolulu: University of Hawaii Press, 1987), 205.

[284]Charles Prebish seems to suggest something similar to this when he calls for more attention to affective component of Buddhist ethics in his "Modern Buddhist Ethics in Asia and America," *The Pacific World* n.s. 8 (1992): 45. Prebish makes use of Harvey B. Aronson's *Love and Sympathy in Theravada Buddhism* (Delhi: Motilal Banarsidass, 1980).

[285]Grosnick, "Nonorigination and *Nirvana* in the Early *Tathāgatagarbha* Literature," *Journal of the International Association of Buddhist Studies* 4/2 (1981): 41.

[286]Although "Shizenbiku" perhaps offers the strongest support for such a reading, other fascicles of Dōgen can be read the same way. Take, for example, the fascicle "Shoakumakusa." As T.P Kasulis puts it, Dōgen uses different understandings of the phrase "Shoakumakusa" to explain the movement in practice from "do no evil," to the "non-production of evil." See his "The Zen Philosopher: A Review Article On Dōgen Scholarship in English," *Philosophy East and West* 28/3 (July 1978): 371-372.

[287]Cook, *How to Raise an Ox*, 55. See Cook's chapter on karma on pages 49-61.

[288]Cook, *Ox*, 58.

[289]Cook, "Dōgen's view of Authentic Selfhood," 136. Or, as Masao Abe puts it, in just slightly different language, karma (the source of evil) is created by grasping and

POIESIS: NON-PRODUCING OF EVIL =?

attachment and can be overcome by abandoning attachment and awakening to the nonsubstantiality of self and objects. Abe discusses karma in "Kenotic God and Dynamic *Śūnyatā*," *The Emptying God*, edited by John Cobb, Jr. and Christopher Ives (Maryknoll NY: Orbis Books 1990), 43-45.

[290]Although the view that dependent arising is primary in Buddhism is most easily sustained with reference to Mādhyamika Buddhism, Japanese scholars in the Critical Buddhism movement read Dōgen through dependent arising as well. The Critical Buddhism movement argues that Buddhist understanding is critical understanding. The essence of true Buddhism is discriminating wisdom, with the emphasis on discrimination. Discriminating wisdom requires difference, not presence. Those in the Critical Buddhism movement suggest that Dōgen had a change of heart about the nature of causality or karmic consequence in Buddhist practice and was in the process of re-writing many of the fascicles of the *Shōbōgenzō* when he died. (Regardless of whether or not this is historically "true," I think this is a very significant contribution on the theological level.) For a summary of the specifics of the argument, see Steven Heine's article "'Critical Buddhism' (*Hihan Bukkyō*) and the Debate Concerning the 75-fascicle and the 12-fascicle *Shōbōgenzō* Texts," *Japanese Religious Studies* 1994 21/1: 37-72.) There would seem to be a potential connection between the Critical Buddhism movement and those who posit an ethic which combines difference (Taylor or Derrida) and otherness (Levinas). Both require the recognition or acceptance of an "absolute other" upon which the construction of the self and any subsequent action is based. For those interested in Buddhist-Jewish/Christian dialogue, this would open up one more line of communication. For others this may be yet another attempt to represent Buddhism in forms compatible with structural frameworks already existing in the Judeo-Christian scholarly tradition. To paraphrase Jikido Takasaki, who may have asked the best question here, Why not just become a Christian? See Paul Swanson's "'Zen is not Buddhism': Recent Japanese Critiques of Buddha Nature," *Numen* 40/2 (1993):138-9.

[291]From the Buddha essence perspective, those who wish to connect Dōgen's Buddhism with Taoism are better off looking for parallels in what some call "religious" or "alchemical" texts rather than early "philosophical" texts (such as the *Tao Te Ching*). See, for example *The Secret of the Golden Flower* (in the translation by Thomas Cleary, New York: Harper Collins, 1991), "Now when you turn the light around to shine inward, [the mind] is not aroused by things; negative energy then stops, and the flower of light radiates a concentrated glow, which is pure positive energy" (41). Or, "Radiant light is the function of the mind, empty silence is the substance of the mind. If there is empty silence without radiant light, the silence is not true silence, the emptiness is not true emptiness -- it is just a ghost cave." The consistent reference in Taoist literature to radiant light (which I would read as the intense luminosity of the non-leaking realm) seems to date back to Chuang Tzu's mention of the "empty chamber where brightness is born" in the discussion on the "fasting of the mind." See *Chuang Tzu: Basic Writings*, translated by Burton Watson (New York: Columbia University Press, 1964), 54. See also *Cultivating Stillness: A Taoist Manual for Transforming*

Body and Mind, trans. Eva Wong (Boston: Shambhala Publications, 1992) and the selections from the Complete Perfection (Quanzhen) school of Taoism in Livia Kohn, ed., *The Taoist Experience: An Anthology* (Albany: State University of New York Press, 1993).

[292]See David Preston's fascinating (and slightly outrageous) article comparing Buddhist practice to becoming a "proficient" marijuana user. "Becoming a Zen Practitioner," *Sociological Analysis* 42/1 (1981): 47-55. Preston focuses on the "physiological" component of Zen practice and suggests that it may be understood to progress in three stages: one learns to do zazen properly so one produces "symptoms"; one learns to identify "symptoms"; one assigns meaning to "symptoms." Preston notes that this is similar to the learning process one goes through in order to smoke marijuana for pleasure (!). He opposes this "physiological" approach to the position that learning to be a Zen practitioner is "taking on a new set of beliefs" or "memorizing a philosophy."

[293]To return to some of the examples used earlier, this play of forces is that which pours out of Heidegger's jug-nothing. "The jug's jug-character consists in the poured gift of the pouring out" (*PLT* 172). This play of forces is also that which is presenced in Heidegger's three dots " . . . ", plays in and out of Taylor's unending vertical "o o o", and is at the origin of the sense which, in the end, turns Orpheus towards Eurydice.

[294]Taylor, *Nots*, 92.

BIBLIOGRAPHY

Abe, Masao. "Kenotic God and Dynamic Śūnyatā," *The Emptying God: A Buddhist-Jewish-Christian Conversation*. Ed. John B. Cobb, Jr., and Christopher Ives. Maryknoll NY: Orbis Books, 1990, 3-65.

_____. *A Study of Dōgen: His Philosophy and Religion*. Ed. Steven Heine. Albany: State University of New York Press, 1992.

_____. *Zen and Western Thought*. Ed. William R. LaFleur. Honolulu: University of Hawaii Press, 1985.

Altizer, Thomas J.J. "Buddhist Emptiness and the Crucifixion of God." *The Emptying God*. Ed. John Cobb Jr. and Christopher Ives. Maryknoll NY: Orbis Books, 1990.

_____. "Emptiness and God." *The Religious Philosophy of Nishitani Keiji*. Ed. Taitetsu Unno. Berkeley: Asian Humanities Press, 1989.

_____. History as Apocalypse. Albany: State University of New York Press, 1985.

_____. *Total Presence: The Language of Jesus and the Language of Today*. New York: Seabury Press, 1980.

Aronson, Harvey B. *Love and Sympathy in Theravada Buddhism*. Delhi: Motilal Banarsidass, 1980.

Auster, Paul. *Leviathan*. New York: Viking Press, 1992.

Balasubramaniam, Arun. "Explaining Strange Parallels: The Case of Quantum Mechanics and Mādhyamika Buddhism," *International Philosophical Quarterly* 32/2, Issue 126 (June 1992): 205-223.

Barrett, William. Ed. *Zen Buddhism: Selected Writings of D.T. Suzuki*. Garden City, NY: Doubleday Anchor Books, 1956.

Bataille, Georges. "The Reasons for Writing a Book." *Yale French Studies 79: Literature and the Ethical Question*. Ed. Claire Nouvet (1991): 11.

Bateson, Gregory. *Steps to an Ecology of Mind*. New York: Ballantine Books, 1972.

_____, et. al. "Toward a Theory of Schizophrenia." *Beyond the Double Bind: Communication and Family Systems, Theories and Techniques with Schizophrenics*. Ed. Milton B. Berger. New York: Brunner/Mazel, 1978.

Baxter, Lewis R. et al. "Caudate Glucose Metabolic Rate Changes With Both Drug and Behavior Therapy for Obsessive-Compulsive

Disorder." *Archives of General Psychiatry* 49 (September 1992): 681-189.

Bernasconi, Robert. "Deconstruction and the Possibility of Ethics." *Deconstruction and Philosophy*. Ed. John Sallis. Chicago: University of Chicago Press, 1987, 122-139.

Bielefeldt, Carl. *Dōgen's Manuals of Zen Meditation*. Berkeley: University of California Press, 1988.

Blakesee, Sandra. "Behavior Therapy Can Change How the Brain Functions, Researchers Say." *New York Times* (September 16, 1992): A20.

Bloom, Harold. *Poetry and Repression: Revisionism from Blake to Stevens*. New Haven: Yale University Press, 1976.

Braidotti, Rosi. *Patterns of Dissonance*. New York: Routledge, 1991.

Brown, Brian Edward. *The Buddha Nature: A Study of the Tathāgatagarbha and Ālayavijñāna*. Delhi: Motilal Banarsidass, 1991.

Campolo, Lisa D. "Derrida and Heidegger: The Critique of Technology and the Call to Care." *Journal of the American Academy of Religion* 53 (September 1985): 431-448.

Caputo, John D. *Against Ethics: Contributions to a Poetics of Obligation with Constant Reference to Deconstruction*. Indianapolis: Indiana University Press, 1993.

_____. "Beyond Aestheticism: Derrida's Responsible Anarchy." *Research in Phenomenology* 18 (1988): 59-73.

_____. *The Mystical Element in Heidegger's Thought*. New York: Fordham University Press, 1986.

Coleridge, Samuel Taylor. *Aids to Reflection*. Ed. Henry Nelson Coleridge. Burlington Vermont: Chauncey Goodrich, 1840.

Conze, Edward, trans. *The Large Sutra on Perfect Wisdom*. Berkeley: University of California Press, 1975.

Cook, Francis. *How To Raise An Ox: Zen Practice as Taught in Zen Master Dōgen's Shōbōgenzō*. Los Angeles: Center Publications, 1978.

_____. "Dōgen's View of Authentic Selfhood and its Socio-ethical Implications." *Dōgen Studies*. Ed. William R. LaFleur. Honolulu: University of Hawaii Press, 1985, 131-149.

_____. "Encounter with Nothing-at-all: Reflections on Hans Waldenfels' Absolute Nothingness." *Buddhist-Christian Studies* 2 (1982): 136-144.

_____. "Just This: Buddhist Ultimate Reality." *Buddhist Christian Studies* 9 (1989): 127-142.

_____. *Sounds of Valley Streams: Enlightenment in Dōgen's Zen.* Albany: State University of New York Press, 1989.

Cousineau, Robert H. *Heidegger, Humanism and Ethics: An Introduction to the Letter on Humanism.* Paris: Beatrice-Nauwelaerts, 1972.

Coward, Harold. *Derrida and Indian Philosophy.* Albany: State University of New York Press, 1990.

Cumming, Robert Denoon. "The Odd Couple: Heidegger and Derrida." *Review of Metaphysics* 34 (March 1981): 487-521.

Dallmayr, Fred. "Nothingness and Sūnyatā: A Comparison of Heidegger and Nishitani." *Philosophy East and West* 42/1 (January 1992): 37-48.

Dean, Thomas. "Masao Abe on Zen and Western Thought." *Eastern Buddhist* n.s.22/2 (Autumn 1989): 48-77.

_____. "Masao Abe on Zen and Western Thought: Part two: First Order Issues." *Eastern Buddhist* n.s. 23/1 (Spring 1990): 79-113.

Deleuze, Gilles. *Logic of Sense.* Trans. Mark Lester with Charles Stivale. New York: Columbia University Press, 1990 (1969).

_____. *Nietzsche and Philosophy.* Trans. Hugh Tomlinson. New York: Columbia University Press, 1983 (1962).

Deleuze, Gilles, and Felix Guattari. *A Thousand Plateaus: Capitalism and Schizophrenia.* Trans. Brian Massumi. Minneapolis: University of Minnesota Press, 1988 (1980).

Derrida, Jacques. "Introduction: Desistance." *Typography: Mimesis, Philosophy, Politics* by Philippe Lacoue-Labarthe. Cambridge Mass: Harvard University Press, 1989, 1-42.

_____. *The Truth of Painting.* Trans. Geoff Bennington and Ian McLeod. Chicago: University of Chicago Press, 1987.

DiCenso, James. "Deconstruction and the Philosophy of Religion: World Affirmation and Critique." *Philosophy of Religion* 31 (1992): 29-43.

Donner, Neal. "Sudden and Gradual Intimately Conjoined: Chih-i's T'ien-t'ai View." *Sudden and Gradual: Approaches to Enlightenment in Chinese Thought.* Ed. Peter N. Gregory. Honolulu: University of Hawaii Press, 1987, 201-226.

Eckel, Malcolm David. "Indian Commentaries of the Heart Sutra: The Politics of Interpretation." *Journal of the International Association of Buddhist Studies* 10/2 (1987): 69-79.

Edmundson, Mark. "The Ethics of Deconstruction." *Michigan Quarterly Review* 27 (Fall 1988): 622-643.

Farias, Victor. *Heidegger and Nazism*. Philadelphia: Temple University Press, 1989.

Faure, Bernard. *Chan Insights and Oversights: An Epistemological Critique of the Chan Tradition*. Princeton: Princeton University Press, 1993.

_____. *The Rhetoric of Immediacy: A Cultural Critique of Chan/Zen Buddhism*. Princeton: Princeton University Press, 1991.

Fox, Douglas A. "Zen and Ethics: Dōgen's Synthesis." *Philosophy East and West* 21 (January 1971): 33-41.

Gasché, Rodolphe. *The Tain of the Mirror: Derrida and the Philosophy of Reflection*. Cambridge Mass: Harvard University Press, 1986.

Gomez, Luis O. "Emptiness and Moral Perfection." Philosophy East and West 23/3 (July 1973): 361-373.

_____. "Indian Materials on the Doctrine of Sudden Enlightenment" *Early Ch'an in China and Tibet*. Ed. Whalen Lai and Lewis R. Lancaster. Berkeley: Asian Humanities Press, 1983, 393-434.

Gowing, Lawrence. "The Logic of Organized Sensations." *Cézanne: the Late Work*. Ed. William Rubin. New York: The Museum of Modern Art, 1977, 55-71.

Grigg, Richard. *Theology as a way of Thinking*. Atlanta: Scholars Press, 1990.

Grosnick, William. "Nonorigination and Nirvāna in the Early Tathāgatagarbha Literature." *Journal of the International Association of Buddhist Studies* 4/2 (1981): 33-43.

Guenther, Herbert V. "Meditation Trends in Early Tibet." *Early Ch'an in China and Tibet*. Ed. Whalen Lai and Lewis R. Lancaster. Berkeley: Asian Humanities Press, 1983, 351-366.

Hakeda, Yoshito S., trans. *The Awakening of Faith, attributed to Aśvaghosa*. New York: Columbia University Press, 1967.

Hanson, Mervin V. "The theoretical basis for Mahāyāna Pluralism in Asanga's 'Mahāyānasamgraha.'" *Journal of the Dharma* 6 (October 1983): 375-383.

Harvey, Irene. *Derrida and the Economy of Différance*. Bloomington: Indiana University Press, 1986.

Hase, Shoto. "Knowledge and Transcendence: Modern Idealist Philosophy and Yogācāra Buddhism." *Japanese Journal of Religious Studies* 11/2-3 (1984): 169-194.

Heidegger, Martin. *An Introduction to Metaphysics*. Trans. Ralph Mannheim. Garden City, NY: Anchor Books, 1961.

_____. *Basic Writings*. Ed. David Farrell Krell. New York: Harper and Row, 1977.

_____. *Discourse on Thinking*. Trans. John M. Anderson and E. Hans Freund. New York: Harper and Row, 1966.

_____. *Early Greek Thinking*. Trans. David Farrell Krell and Frank A. Capuzzi. San Francisco: Harper and Row, 1984.

_____. *Existence and Being*. Ed. Werner Brock. Chicago: Henry Regnery Company, 1965.

_____. *Nietzsche Volume IV: Nihilism*. Trans. Frank A. Capuzzi. Ed. David Farrell Krell. San Francisco: Harper and Row, 1982.

_____. *On the Way to Language*. Trans. Peter D. Hertz. New York: Harper and Row, 1982.

_____. *On Time and Being*. Trans. Joan Stambaugh. New York: Harper and Row, 1972.

_____. *The Piety of Thinking*. Trans. James Hart and John Maraldo. Bloomington: Indiana University Press, 1976.

_____. *Poetry, Language, Thought*. Trans. Albert Hofstadter. New York: Harper and Row, 1975.

_____. *The Question Concerning Technology and Other Essays*. Trans. William Lovitt. New York: Harper and Row, 1977.

_____. *The Question of Being*. Trans. William Kluback and Jean T. Wilde. New York: Twayne Publishers, 1958.

_____. "Thoughts." Trans. Keith Hoeller. *Philosophy Today* 20 (1976): 286-291.

_____. "The Way Back Into the Ground of Metaphysics." *Existentialism from Dostoevsky to Sartre*. Trans. and Ed. Walter Kaufmann. New York: Meridian Books, 1956, 206-221.

_____. *What Is Called Thinking*. Trans. J. Glenn Gray. New York: Harper and Row, 1968.

Heine, Steven. "'Critical Buddhism' (*Hihan Bukkyō*) and the Debate Concerning the 75-fascicle and 12-fascicle *Shōbōgenzō* Texts," *Japanese Journal of Religious Studies* 1994 21/1:37-72.

_____. "Dōgen Casts Off 'What': An Analysis of Shinjin Datsuraku." *Journal of the International Association of Buddhist Studies* 9/1 (1986): 53-70.

_____. *Existential and Ontological Dimensions of Time in Heidegger and Dōgen*. Albany: State University of New York Press, 1985.

_____. "The Flower Blossoms 'Without Why': Beyond the Heidegger-Kuki Dialogue on Contemplative Language." *Eastern Buddhist* n.s. 23 (Autumn 1990): 60-86.

_____. "Multiple Dimensions of Impermanence in Dōgen's `Genjōkōan.'" *Journal of the International Association of Buddhist Studies* 4/2 (1981): 44-62.

_____. "Philosophy for an 'age of death': The critique of science and technology in Heidegger and Nishitani." *Philosophy East and West.* 40/2 (April 1990): 175-193.

_____. "Truth and Method in Dōgen Scholarship: A Review of Recent Works." *Eastern Buddhist* n.s. 20 (Autumn 1987): 128-147.

Hookam, S.K. *The Buddha Within: Tathāgatagarbha Doctrine According to the Shentong Interpretation of the Ratnagotravibhāga.* Albany: State University of New York Press, 1991.

Hopper, Stanley Romaine. *The Way of Transfiguration.* Louisville: Westminster/John Knox Press, 1992.

_____, and David Miller, eds. *Interpretation: The Poetry of Meaning.* New York: Harcourt, Brace and World, Inc., 1967.

Hsiao, Paul Shih-yi. "Heidegger and Our Translation of the Tao Te Ching." *Heidegger and Asian Thought.* Ed. Graham Parkes. Honolulu: University of Hawaii Press, 1987, 93-101.

Huntington, C.W., Jr. *The Emptiness of Emptiness: An Introduction to Early Indian Mādhyamika.* Honolulu: University of Hawaii, 1989.

Ichimura, Shohei. "An Approach to Dōgen's Dialectical Thinking and Method of Instantiation (A Comparative Study of Shō-bō-gen-zō-kū-ge)." *Journal of the International Association of Buddhist Studies* 9/2 (1986): 65-99.

Iida, Shotaro. *Reason and Emptiness: A Study in Logic and Mysticism.* *Tokyo*: The Hokuseido Press, 1980.

Inada, Kenneth K. "The American Involvement with Sūnyatā: Prospects," *Buddhism and American Thinkers.* Ed. K. Inada and N. Jacobson. 1984, 70-88.

Ives, Christopher. "Emptiness: Soteriology and Ethics in Mahāyāna Buddhism." *Concepts of the Ultimate.* Ed. Linda J. Tessier. New York: St. Martin's Press, 113-126.

_____. *Zen Awakening and Society.* Honolulu: University of Hawaii Press, 1992.

Ivy, Marilyn. "Critical Texts, Mass Artifacts: The Consumption of Knowledge in Postmodern Japan." *The South Atlantic Quarterly* 87:3 (Summer 1988): 419-444.

Izutsu, Toshihiko, *Toward a Philosophy of Zen Buddhism*. Boulder: Prajna Press, 1982.

_____, and Hellmut Wilhelm. *On Images: Far Eastern Ways of Thinking*. Dallas: Spring Publications, Inc., 1981.

Kalupahana, David J. *Buddhist Philosophy: A Historical Analysis*. Honolulu: University of Hawaii Press, 1976.

_____. Nagarjuna: *The Philosophy of the Middle Way*. Albany: State University of New York Press, 1986.

Kasulis, T.P. *Zen Action, Zen Person*. Honolulu: University of Hawaii Press, 1985.

_____. "The Two Strands of Nothingness in Zen Buddhism." *International Philosophical Quarterly* 19/1 (March 1979): 61-72.

_____. "The Zen Philosopher: A review article on Dōgen scholarship in English." *Philosophy East and West* 28/3 (July 1978): 353-373.

Kearney, Richard. "Ethics and the Postmodern Imagination." *Thought* 62/244 (March 1987): 39-58.

_____. *The Wake of Imagination: Toward a postmodern culture*. Minneapolis: University of Minnesota Press, 1988.

Kim, Hee-Jin. *Flowers of Emptiness: Selections from Dōgen's Shōbōgenzō*. Lewiston NY: Edwin Mellen Press, 1985.

_____. *Dōgen Kigen: Mystical Realist*. Tucson: University of Arizona Press, Revised edition 1987.

Kimura, Kiyotaka. "The Self in Japanese Buddhism: Focusing on Dōgen," *Philosophy East and West* 41/3 (July 1991): 327-340.

Kiyota, Minoru. "Tathāgatagarbha Thought: A Basis of Buddhist Devotionalism in East Asia." *Japanese Journal of Religious Studies* 12/3 (1985) 207-231.

_____. Ed. *Mahāyāna Buddhist Meditation: Theory and Practice*. Honolulu: University of Hawaii Press, 1978.

Kodera, Takashi James. "The Buddha Nature in Dōgen's Shōbōgenzō." *Japanese Journal of Religious Studies* 4/4 (December 1977): 267-292.

_____. *Dōgen's Formative Years in China*. Boulder: Prajna Press, 1980.

Kuhn, Thomas. *The Essential Tension*. Chicago: University of Chicago Press, 1977.

140 WORKING EMPTINESS

Lacoue-Labarthe, Philippe. *Typography: Mimesis, Philosophy, Politics*. Cambridge Mass.: Harvard University Press, 1989.
LaFleur, William R., ed. *Dōgen Studies*. Honolulu: University of Hawaii Press, 1985.
_____. "Buddhist Emptiness in the Ethics and Aesthetics of Watsuji Tetsuro." *Religious Studies* 14: 237-250.
Leitch, Vincent B. *Deconstructive Criticism: An Advanced Introduction*. New York: Columbia University Press, 1983.
Lingis, Alphonso. "Deleuze on a Deserted Island." *Philosophy and Non-Philosophy since Merleau-Ponty*. Ed. Hugh J. Silverman. New York: Routledge, 1988.
Loy, David. "Indra's Postmodern Net," *Philosophy East and West* 43/3 (July 1993): 481-510.
Magliola, Robert. *Derrida on the Mend*. West Lafayette, Indiana: Purdue University Press, 1984.
Marx, Werner. *Is There a Measure On Earth? Foundations for a Nonmetaphysical Ethics*. Chicago: University of Chicago Press, 1987 (1983).
Massumi, Brian. *A user's guide to Capitalism and Schizophrenia: Deviations from Deleuze and Guattari*. Cambridge, Massachusetts: MIT Press, 1992.
Masunaga, Reiho. *A Primer of Soto Zen: A translation of Dōgen's Shōbōgenzō Zuimonki*. Honolulu: University of Hawaii Press, 1975.
Matilal, Bimal Krishna. "Is *Prasanga* a Form of Deconstruction?" *Journal of Indian Philosophy* 20 (1992): 345-362.
McLean, M.D. "The Meaning of Sūnya in the Teaching of Nāgārjuna." *The Scottish Journal of Religious Studies* 7/1 (Spring 1986): 29-50.
Meyer, Eric C. "Thomas J.J. Altizer's Construction of Ultimate Meaning." *Ultimate Reality and Meaning* 1 (1978): 258-277.
Michelfelder, Diane. "Derrida and the Ethics of the Ear," *The Question of the Other*. Ed. Arleen B. Dallery and Charles E. Scott. Albany: State University of New York Press, 1989, 47-54.
Miller, David L. *Hells and Holy Ghosts: A Theopoetics of Christian Belief*. Nashville: Abingdon Press, 1989.
Motte, Warren F. Jr. "Clinamen Redux," *Comparative Literature Studies* 23 (1986): 263-281.
Nagao, Gadjin. *The Foundational Standpoint of Mādhyamika Philosophy*. *Albany*: State University of New York Press, 1989.

_____. *Mādhyamika and Yogācāra*. Albany: State University of New York Press, 1991.

Nagatomo, Shigenori. *Attunement Through the Body*. Albany: State University of New York Press, 1992

_____. "An Analysis of Dōgen's 'Casting off Body and Mind.'" *International Philosophical Quarterly* 27/3, Number 107 (September 1987): 227-242.

Nishitani, Keiji. *Religion and Nothingness*. Berkeley: University of California Press, 1983.

Odin, Steve. "Kenosis as a Foundation for Buddhist Christian Dialogue: The Kenotic Buddhology of Nishida and Nishitani of the Kyoto School in relation to the Kenotic Christology of Thomas J.J. Altizer." *Eastern Buddhist* n.s. 20/1 (1987): 34-61.

Olivier, G. "Derrida, Art and Truth." *Journal of Literary Studies* 3 (1985): 27-38.

Ost, Ruth. "Changing Frames: A Critique of Prescriptions for Personal Transformation in the Theories of C.G. Jung, James W. Fowler and Albert C. Barnes." Ph.D. dissertation, Temple University, 1994.

Paul, Diana Mary. *The Buddhist Feminine Ideal: Queen Śrimālā and the Tathāgatagarbha*. Missoula Montana: Scholars Press, 1980.

Parkes, Graham, ed. *Heidegger and Asian Thought*. Honolulu: University of Hawaii Press, 1987.

Phillips, Stephen H. "Nishitani's Buddhist Response to 'Nihilism.'" *Journal of the American Academy of Religion* LV/1: 75-104.

Pilgrim, Richard B. "Intervals (Ma) in Space and Time: Foundations for a Religio-Aesthetic Paradigm in Japan." *History of Religions* 25/3 (1986): 255-277.

Prebish, Charles. "Modern Buddhist Ethics in Asia and America." The *Pacific World* n.s. 8 (1992): 40-47.

Preston, David. "Becoming a Zen Practitioner." *Sociological Analysis* 42/1 (1981): 47-55.

Ramanan, K. Venkata. *Nāgārjuna's Philosophy as Presented in the Mahā-Prajñāpāramita-Sastra*. Rutland Vermont: Charles E. Tuttle Co., 1966. Reprinted in Delhi by Motilal Banarsidass, 1975.

Richards, Glyn. "*Śūnyatā*: Objective Referent or Via Negativa." *Religious Studies* 14, 251-260.

Richardson, William J. "Heidegger, Truth and Politics," *Ethics and Danger.* Ed. Arleen B. Dallery and Charles E. Scott. Albany: State University of New York Press, 1992, 11-24.

Rubin, William, ed. *Cézanne: The Late Work.* New York: The Museum of Modern Art, 1977.

Ruegg, David Seyfort. "On the *Dge Lugs Pa* Theory of the *Tathāgatagarbha.*" *Pratidanam.* Ed. J.C. Heesterman et. al. The Hague: Mouton, 1968, 500-509.

_____. "The *Jo Nan Pas*: A School of Buddhist Ontologists According to the *GRUB MTHA SEL GYI ME LON.*" *Journal of the American Oriental Society* 83 (1963): 73-91.

_____. *The Literature of the Mādhyamika School of Philosophy in India.* Weisbaden: Otto Harrassowitz, 1981.

Ruf, Henry. "The Origin of the Debate over Ontotheology and Deconstruction in the Texts of Wittgenstein and Derrida." *Religion, Ontotheology and Deconstruction.* New York: Paragon House, 1989, 3-42.

Scharlemann, Robert. "Being Open and Thinking Theologically." *Unfinished . . . : Essays in Honor of Ray Hart.* Ed. Mark Taylor. Chico: Scholars Press, 1981, 111-124.

_____. *Negation and Theology.* Charlottesville: The University Press of Virginia, 1992.

_____, ed. *Theology At The End Of The Century.* Charlottesville: The University Press of Virginia, 1990.

Schurmann, Reiner. *Heidegger on Being and Acting: From Principles to Anarchy.* Bloomington: Indiana University Press, 1990 (1987).

_____. "The Loss of the Origin in Sōtō Zen and in Meister Eckhart," *The Thomist* 42/2 (1978): 281-312.

Scott, Charles E. *The Question of Ethics: Nietzsche, Foucault, Heidegger.* Bloomington: Indiana University Press, 1990.

Shaner, David Edward. *The Bodymind Experience in Japanese Buddhism: A Phenomenological Study of Kūkai and Dōgen.* Albany: State University of New York Press, 1985.

Shaw, Miranda. *Passionate Enlightenment: Women in Tantric Buddhism.* Princeton: Princeton University Press, 1994.

Sharf, Robert H. "The Zen of Japanese Nationalism," *History of Religions* 33/1 (1993): 1-43.

Stambaugh, Joan. *Impermanence is Buddha-nature: Dōgen's Understanding of Temporality*. Honolulu: University of Hawaii Press, 1990.

_____. *The Finitude of Being*. Albany: State University of New York Press, 1992.

Streng, Frederick. "Three religious ontological claims: 'being-itself,' 'nothingness exists within somethingness,' and 'the field of emptiness.'" *Traditions in Contact and Change*. ed. P. Slater and D. Wiebe, 1983, 249-266.

_____. *Emptiness: A Study in Religious Meaning*. New York: Abingdon Press, 1967.

Swanson, Paul L. "'Zen is not Buddhism': Recent Japanese Critiques of Buddha Nature," *Numen* 40/2 (1993): 115-149.

Takasaki, Jikido. *An Introduction to Buddhism*. Trans. Rolf W. Giebel. Tokyo: The Tōhō Gakkai, 1987.

_____. *A Study on the Ratnagotravibhāga (Uttaratantra): Being a Treatise on Tathāgatagarbha Theory of Mahāyāna Buddhism*. Rome: Is.M.E.O. Serie Orientale Roma Vol. XXXIII, 1966.

Tanahashi, Kazuaki, ed., *Moon in a Dewdrop: Writings of Zen Master Dōgen*. San Francisco: North Point Press, 1985.

Taylor, Mark C. *Altarity*. Chicago: University of Chicago Press, 1987.

_____. "Altizer's Originality: A Review Essay." *Journal of the American Academy of Religion* LII/3 (1984): 569-584.

_____. *Deconstructing Theology*. Chico: Scholars Press, 1982.

_____. *Disfiguring*. Chicago: University of Chicago Press, 1992.

_____. *Erring: A Postmodern A/theology*. Chicago: University of Chicago Press, 1984.

_____. "nO nOt nO." *Derrida and Negative Theology*. Ed. Harold Coward and Toby Forshay. Albany: State University of New York Press, 1992, 167-198.

_____. *Nots*. Chicago: University of Chicago Press, 1993.

_____. "Orthodox-y (-) Mending." [A review essay on *Derrida on the Mend*] *Thought* 61/240 (March 1986): 162-171.

_____. *Tears*. Albany: State University of New York Press, 1990.

Tournier, Michel. *Friday*. Trans. Norman Denny. New York: Pantheon Books, 1985 (1967).

Tuck, Andrew P. *Comparative Philosophy and the Philosophy of Scholarship: On the Western Interpretation of Nāgārjuna.* New York: Oxford Press, 1990.

Unno, Mark. "The Divine in the Contemporary World: A Conversation with Nishitani Keiji, Kawai Hayao and David Miller." *Kyoto Journal* 8 (Fall 1988): 16-22.

Van de Koppel, Jan M.H. *A Developmental Study of the Biaka Pygmies and the Bangandu.* Lisse: Swets and Zeitlinger, 1983.

Victoria, Daizen. "Japanese Corporate Zen," *Bulletin of Concerned Asian Scholars* 12 (1980): 61-68.

Vycinas, Vincent. *Earth and Gods: An Introduction to the Philosophy of Martin Heidegger.* The Hague, Netherlands: Martinus Nijhoff, 1969.

Waddell, Norman. "Dōgen's *Hōkyōki*," Eastern Buddhist n.s. Part One 10/2 (October 1977): 102-139. Part Two 11/1 (May 1978): 66-84.

_____, and Masao Abe, trans. "Dōgen's *Shōbōgenzō: Zenki* 'Total Dynamic Working' and *Shōji* 'Birth and Death.'" *Eastern Buddhist* n.s. 5/1 (1972): 70-80.

_____. "'One Bright Pearl': Dōgen's *Shōbōgenzō: Ikka Myōju*," *Eastern Buddhist* n.s. 4/2 (1971): 108-118.

_____. "*Shōbōgenzō Genjōkōan.*" *Eastern Buddhist* n.s. 5/2 (October 1972): 129-140.

Waldenfels, Hans. *Absolute Nothingness: Foundations for Buddhist-Christian Dialogue.* New York: Paulist Press, 1980 (1976).

Wapner, Seymour and Jack Demick, eds. *Field Dependence-Independence: Cognitive Styles Across the Life Span.* Hillsdale NJ: Lawrence Erlbaum Associates, 1991.

Wayman, Alex. "The Mahāsamghika and the Tathāgatagarbha (Buddhist Doctrinal History, Study 1)." *Journal of the International Association of Buddhist Studies* 1/1 (1978): 35-50.

Wayman, Alex and Hideko. *The Lion's Roar of Queen Śrimālā.* New York: Columbia University Press, 1974.

Whitehill, James. "Is There a Zen Ethic?" *Eastern Buddhist* n.s. 20 (Spring 1987): 9-33.

Williams, Paul. *Mahāyāna Buddhism: The Doctrinal Foundations.* New York: Routledge, 1989.

_____. "On the Interpretation of Mādhyamika Thought." (Review article of *The Emptiness of Emptiness* by C.W. Huntington Jr.). *Journal of Indian Philosophy* 19 (1991): 191-218.

Winquist, Charles. *Epiphanies of Darkness: Deconstruction in Theology.* Philadelphia: Fortress Press, 1986.

Wittgenstein, Ludwig. *Last Writings, Volume I: Preliminary Studies for Part II of Philosophical Investigations. Ed. G.H. Wright and Heikki Nyman.* Chicago: University of Chicago Press, 1990.

_____. *Philosophical Investigations.* (Second edition) Oxford: B. Blackwell, 1958.

Wolin, Richard, ed. *The Heidegger Controversy: A Critical Reader.* New York: Columbia University Press, 1991.

Wright, Dale S. "Doctrine and the concept of truth in Dōgen's Shōbōgenzō." *Journal of the American Academy of Religion* 54/2 (Summer 1986): 257-277.

_____. "Rethinking Transcendence: The Role of Language in Zen Experience." *Philosophy East and West* 42/1 (January 1992): 113-138.

Wyschogrod, Edith. "On Deconstructing Theology: A Symposium on Erring: A Postmodern A/Theology." *Journal of the American Academy of Religion* LIV/3 (1986): 523-557.

_____. *Saints and Postmodernism: Revisioning Moral Philosophy.* Chicago: University of Chicago Press, 1990.

_____. "Theology in the Wake of the Other." (A review essay on *Altarity*) *Journal of the American Academy of Religion* LVI/1 (1988): 115-130.

Yampolsky, Philip B. *The Platform Sutra of the Sixth Patriarch.* New York: Columbia University Press, 1967.

Yeshe, Lama. *Introduction to Tantra: A Vision of Totality.* Compiled and ed. Jonathan Landaw. London: Wisdom, 1987.

Yokoi, Yūhō, trans. *The Shōbō-genzō.* Tokyo: Sankibo Buddhist Book-store, 1986.

_____. *Zen Master Dōgen: An Introduction with Selected Writings.* Tokyo: Weatherhill, 1976.

Yuasa, Yasuo. T*he Body: Toward an Eastern Mind-Body Theory*, ed. T.P. Kasulis. Trans. Nagatomo Shigenori and T.P. Kasulis. Albany: State University of New York Press, 1987.

_____. "The Encounter of Modern Japanese Philosophy with Heidegger," *Heidegger and Asian Thought*, ed. Graham Parkes. Honolulu: University of Hawaii Press, 1990, 155-174.

Zimmerman, Michael E. *Eclipse of the Self: The Development of Heidegger's Concept of Authenticity*. Athens: Ohio University Press, 1981.

_____. "The Limitations of Heidegger's Ontological Aestheticism." *The Southern Journal of Philosophy* 28, Supplement (1989): 183-189.

Portions of this book appear in Newman Robert Glass, "Splits and Gaps in Buddhism and Postmodern Theology," *Journal of the American Academy of Religion* (forthcoming, 1996).